RESTORATION
TOTALLY

RESTORATION

TOTALLY

YVONNE MALLORY

CREATION
HOUSE
A STRANG COMPANY

RESTORATION TOTALLY by Yvonne Mallory
Published by Creation House
A Strang Company
600 Rinehart Road
Lake Mary, Florida 32746
www.creationhouse.com

Unless otherwise noted, all Scripture quotations are from the New King James Version of the Bible. Copyright © 1979, 1980, 1982 by Thomas Nelson, Inc., publishers. Used by permission.

Scripture quotations marked KJV are from the King James Version of the Bible.

Cover design by Terry Clifton

Library of Congress Control Number: 2005930192
International Standard Book Number: 1-59185-902-6

First Edition

05 06 07 08— 987654321
Printed in the United States of America

This book is dedicated to my children, Mable, James Jr., Keren, and Emmanuel who, while I tried to give to them everything, have in turn given the most to me: neverending love, trust, and strength because of their devotion.

Also, to my sisters, Doris, Audrey, Mary, Barbara and Mable who have always demonstrated their belief in me and God's call upon my life.

And to those who provided the challenges and obstacles for which I had to overcome. You were used to help make me who I am today, for this I say thank you.

To my friend Gloria who had always been there; nearly thirty years through all the cups of coffee with all the tears and never questioning.

And lastly, but not least at all...

To my wonderful husband and man of God, Gregory Mallory, whom God has placed into my life to allow the wonderful force of divine restoration to be lived and exemplified and shared. Thanks for your love, your faith, and for your strong belief in me as a wife and as a woman of God.

Acknowledgments

I MUST WITHOUT DOUBT acknowledge Drs. Fred and Betty Price of Crenshaw Christian Center, Los Angeles, California, for their godly lives and for how they have taught me about faith in God. As my spiritual mom and dad they have influenced my life in many ways so that I can be used by God to influence the lives of others. God brought us together by His divine order and for this I will always remain grateful. I am appreciative of their trust and belief in the God within me. Without them this book would not be possible, but because of their love for God's people it can now be shared. Thank you both from deep within my heart.

Contents

Foreword

*R*ESTORATION *TOTALLY* SHOULD be read by every Christian. If one does not need it for himself or herself, they should have it to help someone else through their challenges. It is a story of victory and triumph over the circumstances of life. Being responsible for the women's work in my congregation, I come in contact with hundreds of women who have issues. They suffer from rejection, abandonment, loneliness, abuse, molestation, mistreatment, rape, low self-esteem, and hurts of all kinds. Minister Yvonne Mallory shares in her book how to overcome all of these negative challenges or issues that one may face. She faced many hurts, rejection, racism, mistreatment, etc. in her own life for years until she realized that through much prayer and study of the Word that God had already provided the way out for her. She had to learn how to access her answer by faith. She shares in a way to let others know that God is there for them and how they can overcome every challenge they are faced with. She is now living an overcoming and victorious life, a life of peace and joy in the Holy Spirit. That life of freedom is available for every person who desires to be free. You will find out how to have this life by reading *Restoration Totally.*

—BETTY R. PRICE, D.D.

Preface

…the eyes of your understanding being enlightened;
that you may know what is the hope of His calling,
what are the riches of the glory of His inheritance in the
saints, and what is the exceeding greatness of His power
toward us who believe, according to the working of His
mighty power.

—Ephesians 1:18–19

THESE DYNAMIC, SPIRITUALLY power-packed words were
spoken by the apostle Paul to the Church at Ephesus while
he was still in prison. How do we in times of great challenges
only focus on the immeasurable exceeding greatness of His
power? You can only do this by allowing your heart and mind
to take a faith journey into greater spiritual dimensions. Today,
we are privileged as never before to embrace all God truly has
made available to each of us. Yet why is lack all around us and
we too live in such lack at times? God has spoken and said that
we have all things pertaining to life and godliness. We still say
to God we are waiting on Him to give us all things. Something
is dreadfully wrong. Since He is a God who cannot lie, the

\ust be with us. Do we know how to allow His bless-
_ .. burst or storm into our lives? Blessings are supposed to
run us down and overtake us. Understanding how to move
into new dimensions requires a deep thought process. When
we think of dimension we know it to be the area by which
something expands or reaches, or the area covered in the natural sense. Length and width is the most common way man
thinks today when we focus on dimensions naturally. Now, let
us add to these two dimensions another natural dimension,
depth or thickness. In our earthly natural dimensions this is
what we have, length, width, depth. This is how we get 3-D.
There are other words within the English language that are
synonyms for these, such as height, breadth, or thickness, but
it is all the same. The fourth dimension, when added to the
natural three dimensions, takes us into the extraordinary. I
am not talking about some hocus-pocus stuff; I am speaking
of where God has always existed in the spiritual realm. The
spirit realm is the most powerful. We as humans just thought
we came up with the first, second, and third dimensions. In
the beginning where God existed was the first dimension. It is
there and only there that our natural problems and situations
find unusual resolve. It is only when we *reach* far beyond the
size of our battles that we can touch the fourth dimension or
a realm only occupied by divine resources. Mountain-moving
faith is faith that reaches beyond the natural dimensions of
our situations and touches the heart of God. We have heard
of actual races where the runner engaged in speed that defied
human abilities or set world records. Well, in the spiritual God
wants us to run not with human ability but run the race that is
set before us with faith. It is a faith battle. There were biblical
characters that had no regard for the natural height, width, or
depth of their circumstances. Joseph was one such character.

He was out of touch with the natural aspects and events of his journey. He could not even relate to the thoughts his brothers had after the death of their father. Joseph wept because they thought he would seek to do them harm or take revenge after their father's death. Joseph had reached far beyond where their minds existed. The brothers did not really know who Joseph truly was within. I can think of two significant times in the Bible when Joseph cried. Joseph cried when his brothers were returned to him and he made himself known to them. He cried also when he realized that although they were with him they did not know who he was. How sad it is for us to be with God and yet not know who He really is, like the brothers of Joseph. Think of how Jesus felt when He said, "O Jerusalem, Jerusalem!" We must realize who He is and the power of His resurrection if we are ever to go into higher spiritual awareness or to a higher dimension guided by faith.

The challenge is for each of us to reach so high in faith that the spiritual realm takes over totally and nothing is impossible for us. Then and only then can we say as the apostle Paul that neither height nor depth, nor any other creature, can separate us from God. Do a faith-reach so high that you catapult your life from despair to repair and from lack to overflowing. You will know within your spirit when new dimensions have been embraced. Since man's spirit is the candle of the Lord, God will light your spirit with a witness. You will ask yourself the question, "How did I get from yonder place to where I am today? How was the sycamine tree rooted up from my life and planted in the sea as Jesus said in Luke 17:6?" When the apostles said, "Lord increase our faith" (Luke 17:5), Jesus answered by telling them the results of having a little bit of mustard-seed faith. Using that mustard-seed faith can take you far into a new dimension. Begin right now to cut your natural senses off from your situations no matter how bad things seem. The enemy uses many different tools to outwit God's people. Looking at our problems with the natural eye is a trick from the enemy. But we are not ignorant of Satan's devices. You will only get God's best when your faith surpasses the level your problems live at. Get above your problems and above the storms. Allow your faith to soar you into a new realm of breakthrough. When we move into the spiritual dimension it is where the immeasurable lives and happens. This is where Isaiah looked and proclaimed, later confirmed by Paul, that "eye hath not seen, nor ear heard, neither have entered into the heart of man, the things which God hath prepared for them that love Him" (1 Cor. 2:9). The prophet Isaiah added that there was never a God that works like He does on behalf of His people. Move out of your old place where doubt, dismay, and fear are your occupants. Move into new dimensions where God declares He will do a new thing and where you experience double for your sorrow. New things await you as you press on to a new spiritual dimension.

Introduction

For I know the thoughts that I think toward you, says the LORD, thoughts of peace and not of evil, to give you a future and a hope.

—JEREMIAH: 29:11

JEREMIAH GIVES THIS wonderful proclamation of restoration from the mouth of God. He explains to God's people that although you have been in bondage and have lost everything, God has great plans for you. Jeremiah was announcing that the captivity was going to end and God would visit with good and only good plans for their natural life and spiritual well being. Many of us today seem to not know that the captivity has ended. Many years have passed and we are not walking in the restoration intended, nor do many of us even realize that wholeness awaits us if we seek it.

God's people spent seventy years in captivity and experienced a tremendous struggle to get back to where they should be, but God had promised what He would do after the seventy years.

> For thus says the LORD: After seventy years are completed at Babylon, I will visit you and perform My good word toward you, and cause you to return to this place.
> —JEREMIAH 29:10

Israel's struggle was in believing and taking hold of this planned restoration for their lives. Many of us are at this same juncture in life today. We can't seem to take hold of the wholeness through faith in God that He has already made available to us through His Son, Jesus. We are still toiling and fighting with taking God at His word that restoration is ours. It has already been made available to us no matter how severe the circumstances. We need to be uncomfortable with our own deficiencies and lack of faith, but because we hide them very well we don't truly address them. Betrayals, hurt, guilt, shame, lack of success, and brokenness along with "what I should have done" and "what I could have done" will plague us to our graves if we don't do something divine about it. Yes, I know things have crushed, hurt, and nearly crippled us all, but there is a way to not allow yourself to live in the memories of those happenings.

What we see many times as the beginning of a problem is really the result of deeper situations. Often, situations of bondage and captivity happen in stages. The bondage does not occur all at once. Certain components of our lives are bit by bit and little by little taken over by the enemy. Many times this happens so smoothly and with such deception that we don't even realize we have entered into a captive state. We are not who God intended us to be. We are not operating as the Spirit of the Living God designed us to. This is the whole idea of the enemy: to render us useless and void of the power of God that makes us effective in His kingdom.

For about forty years the prophet Jeremiah told and prophesied of a sure destruction that God's people were directly headed for. Jeremiah also was key in revealing the restoration triumph in specific order for captivity to cease. But the restoration process was revealed even before the Babylonian seizure happened. That is just like God: He always prepares the end before the beginning. He knew the bondage would occur so He gave us the solution. Today, we must stop the destruction that today's bonda ... rings with it.

> forth His hand and touched my
> said to me: "Behold, I have put
> outh. See, I have this day set you
> ver the kingdoms, to root out and
> oy and to throw down, to build
>
> —Jeremiah 1:9–10

d revealed to me lead to freedom
ey will be clearly outlined in this
tep, one by one, as we walk our way
e six steps to recovery now!

Chapter 1

The Storm Begins

Many times a storm begins long before it is visible to the naked eye. Trouble reveals itself in many different ways and may have been lurking in our lives long before we ever began to recognize the warning signs. How we handle relationships can tell us a lot about who we really are. Most who think of themselves as strong, independent, and sharp often fold during extreme turmoil and become weaker than they want to admit.

Very early in my youth, mounds of insecurities and distortions about life began taking form. My family grew up in core ghetto, West Side Chicago, Illinois. Life was not much, nor did I expect much from it. You were glad just to get along from day to day. If someone treated you half decent you thought it to be a swell thing. I never learned to set higher expectations for others or myself. Originally, I thought my problems began when I first found out I had married into a relationship that held more horror than what I actually knew existed in the world. I was so young and undeveloped that I did not know such emotional and mental lows existed. Abuse comes in all shapes, colors, and dimensions. I was so wrong about how I thought the world was really put together. I thought that when my marriage of thirty years ended that I could look back and see where the actual problems all began. My mind's eye was not capable of allowing me to look far enough back or deep enough into when things really went wrong. I needed a different method to see the heart of my problems and not physical ability. When your world falls apart and you are betrayed over and over again you try to improve yourself and identify your own ills.

Betrayal comes in many shapes but always ends up doing the same type of damage. If you have ever faced relationship betrayal, or have been severely handicapped in life because of something done to you, it leaves you with debris and ruined areas in your life. However, many times what we fail to see is that the ills are not within us but within the person committing the horrors toward us. Now this does not mean that we don't need correction. It does mean that many times we believe the fault to be in us when we actually need to understand that people have many different issues that drive them to harm others. I am not saying that we don't many times, in some sort of way, contribute to our circumstances. Sometimes we do contribute to our issues and circumstances, but how the other person responds is with them and not with us. When we are cheated, abused, or betrayed in a relationship it should tell us that the other person involved had issues with life that they could not handle. Instead, we look for what issues we have. This is the wrong conclusion.

For many of the thirty years of my marriage, I aggressively pursued locating my errors that had caused this world of nightmares. My very strong will to survive and not fail at anything caused a greater failure that I was not aware of. I was failing at the principles of life God had always said I was entitled to.

You see, a person's drive can be so strong that it works against them. All human-driven abilities should be channeled in the right direction or the result can be disastrous, as in my case.

I married very, very young. I was just out of high school when I moved into a torturous and co-dependent situation. I don't even truly remember just when the days and nights of pain, disloyalty, and bitter treatment began. All I can recall is that there were years of tears; and I literally mean years. You see, I did not understand life enough nor was I developed to the point to even help myself. It seemed many times it was only God and me. The strength He gave me to withstand the hardest blows was all I had. It took what seemed forever for me to learn that you cannot change other people. People cheat, lie, steal, and degrade themselves along with embarrassing their families because that is who they are. They must obey their father, the devil.

There were nights and days when I would encounter situations that no one should be forced to live through, but I was determined to let none of it break me down. People often make decisions about how they want to live and whom they want to live it with. When we are not a part of those plans sometimes we receive more good from it than we think. I praise God for giving me the victory. Because of the strong person I was I thought that life was trying beat me and I wasn't going to let it. On the outside I weathered my storms quite well, but on the inside the situation was nearly killing me. In fact, many people close to me feared the worst outcome for me since my emotional state was being hit so hard. I faced a multitude of very difficult events time after time and I really did not know how to handle the horror of it all.

During much of this time I was not perfect as an individual, but I thought I was. I also began to blame myself. I tried to improve in areas that were impossible under the current of emotional havoc I was in. I spent nights afterward visualizing over and over every picture in my head, things that no wife or husband should even think about. My very active mind caused me to even go further into torturing myself because I had not learned how to forget those things as I later learned through God's Word to do. I thought of my children and what to do all the time. First one child and then two, three, and four. How could I tell my children that I had failed at anything? I could not, so I stayed handicapped in the mire of hatred. I was one of the best enablers you have ever met. I enabled the person to send these things into my life.

There is one thing I did not realize that I want my readers to understand: you can either do now what you need to do for your life as God directs, or you will have to do it later at a much greater cost. Here is what I mean. During the early years of my marriage I had no business staying with anyone who treated me in such a low-down way. However, for all the wrong reasons I stayed—call it pride, call it wanting to win, call it stupidity, or call it anything you like—I stayed. I would look into the eyes of extremely devastating events and go home afterwards and pretend everything was all right. There came a time in my life when God caught up with my senses and I had to do what I did not do earlier. It is just that when I finally did it, thirty years later, it cost me so much, much more. In fact, had it not been for a faithful God it would have cost me my life.

Unbeknownst to me until later years, my oldest daughter had begun to make plans on my committal to be institutionalized due to my situation. She felt I was headed toward a mental or emotional breakdown, and it could not be avoided. I appeared OK on the outside. However, while she observed what life was throwing at me and how I accepted it and bounced back, she knew her mom could do nothing but breakdown and end up having to have someone take of her. She felt responsible to find the best home and care for me and be prepared when it happened. It never happened. I clung to God with every breath in my body and I learned of how He loved me so very much. Even while blaming God and becoming angry with God for doing these things to me I learned that the only thing God did to me was carry me through the storm. I began to learn that God does not do evil and harm to us. God wrapped His loving arms around me and waited thirty long years for me to recognize who I am in Him.

While we should indeed look at what we could do better, we must never forget that life is choice-driven for us all; including the person or persons that made you a victim. Usually, our real problems lie in the fact that we allow the abuse, as I did for many, many years. I was the victim of much extreme emotional and mental torture for most of the thirty years I was married. My ridiculous reaction to remedy the constant displays of disloyalties by my own strength nearly killed me and tried to send me to an early grave. The many experiences and encounters of actual betrayal situations should have brought awareness, but instead I was a prisoner blinded of my own worth. Nearly thirty years of sadness, pain, grief, and sure doom; it is near shocking how I did this to myself. I was as blind as Balaam when he mounted his donkey to go to Balak about cursing the children of Israel.

> Then the Lord opened Balaam's eyes, and he saw...
> —NUMBERS 22:31

Balak kept asking Balaam to curse what was blessed and I kept asking God for a blessing for what had become cursed. Keep in mind, some situations are touched by the hand of

God, and they turn into a blessed event. However, you and I sometimes seek a fix in the wrong way, as it was in my case.

God is the only one who can reveal to us the true assessment of the different issues. We all know that God is the God of restoration, and that is what I am writing about. We must live close to God in order to know what the restoration applies to. Sometimes we are trying to restore people and a situation and God merely wants to restore us. If God can restore us to where we need to be, it in turn helps any matter. Had I allowed God to work restoration on me I would have viewed things differently. My awareness from God would have had a positive effect on things. Instead, I did not realize God was not trying to take anything from me, He was trying to get something to me. I was too full of hurt, pain, and determination to prove the world wrong to see my own need for self-worth and care the way God intended.

How could a very successful, bright, intelligent person allow repeated betrayals before her very eyes and act as if what she had just encountered was nothing at all? Why did I not realize that I could not provide the help that was needed for the other person? My past molded my future and I was able to accept the horrors I lived with night after night. My children cried with me many nights. It was also destroying them, but I did not even recognize they needed my help. I was so lost in my own world of pain that I was not able to help anyone, not even my four children. How sad!

The children of Israel were this way. They just messed things up not knowing who they really were to God. God loves His children so much and never intended for us to live in a less than godly state of happiness. The children of Israel got so far away from what God intended for them that it took years to get back. Think about this: God with a mighty hand delivers you and me from sin just as He delivered the children of Israel with a mighty hand. After a miraculous deliverance we surrender to satanic strongholds that prevent us from enjoying the God of our salvation. Many of the children of Israel got so far away from God's plan that they never found it again.

> But with most of them God was not well pleased, for their bodies were scattered in the wilderness.
> —1 Corinthians 10:5

That is where some of us are headed if we do not awaken to who we really are. We are going to die in the wilderness of our own mess. We shake hands with the devil and come out swinging. We don't have to die in the wilderness of our situations and storms.

Whatever your storm is, don't die in it. You can wander in the wilderness and be lost while the escape is right there. Joshua and Caleb did not die in the wilderness because they believed the God of their fathers. They said they were more than able to defeat giants. They acknowledged that their adversaries were truly giants and bigger than they, but Joshua and Caleb knew that God was with them. Don't wander fifteen, twenty, thirty, or any number of years in the wilderness through hopelessness. Seek God and He will answer you for your problems. Know who you are in God. Start on a path to restoration today. Sometimes you don't have to leave a situation to be restored, but the situation has to leave you for you to be restored.

Let me tell you one true story of very embarrassing nights to help you see what the enemy will do to you if you allow him. I tell this story very reluctantly because I never wanted these weaknesses to be known. It is very embarrassing for me. But I share it to help someone else get free from the strongholds of the enemy and the decay it brings to self-worth. But you have to know you need restoration first. Several nights passed and I was always home alone night and day during certain periods. My eldest daughter began to figure that the only person sleeping in the house with them each night was Mom. So the girls would inquire of me why I was alone for long periods. I would not lie to them so I learned how to give clever answers. I learned to look at the clock each morning and, since I knew my husband would go to the office from wherever he lodged, I learned to tell the kids that he is at work now. For many years I thought I hid this from the children by just saying the next morning that their father was at work. I decided sometimes to prove this and upon verifying with a phone call I continued in my world of pretense.

Well, as the children grew they put two and two together, and they soon told me, "Mom, it's OK, you don't have to say that anymore. We know you were alone as we slept." This nearly destroyed them as well because now they had to face the harsh reality that I had concealed for so long. I taught them the wrong things. I should have called it what it really was. The home situation almost caused one of the children to end their life. They could not live in the mix-up, mess-up my decisions put us in. God was merciful and we are all well in the Lord today. Those were very scary times for the children and me. I screamed at man, God, and the world from within my spirit when I was in that nasty storm. I screamed many nights for just a breath of fresh air. I needed the pain to stop.

All God wanted me to do was to recognize He did not put me in the wilderness. I put myself in the wilderness with the decisions I made. When we make wilderness decisions we get wilderness results. When we make crossing-the-Red-Sea-decisions we can remember what Moses said, "For the Egyptians whom you see today, you shall see again no more forever" (Exod. 14:13). What am I saying? No one other than God can tell you when to leave a situation, but you should be able to tell yourself when to change a situation. Every time the children of Israel saw another so-called storm arising they cried and murmured and complained. That is what kept them in the wilderness. They could have just stepped out of the wilderness simply through obedience and faith.

That is what it takes. Simply, faith and obedience can change the direction of the storm. Whereas it was directed straight at you, the storm takes another course because you now know who you are in God. Will it be the wilderness forever or will you no longer see and hear the madness, the Egyptians, and the turmoil and go ahead and cross the scary Red Sea that is before you?

Chapter 2

The Rage to Survive

THE MOST PROFOUND spiritual crisis known to mankind many times is that of the period following extreme bondage. Think of any period of bondage or captivity and how even a more profound crisis was at hand when the captivity in the physical form no longer existed. Whether it is Old Testament Israel, the Jews following the holocaust, or African Americans' slavery period, the many years following the cease of the physical captivity proved to be a more profound crisis that they had to face. This is because of the valuable inner qualities that are destroyed during actual bondage. We face an even greater problem to be restored after the storm because of the storm's destructiveness. Even today many are still not able to overcome the damage from many years past and pass these crippling effects on to generation after generation. They, as I did, have experienced a period in which their faith about life had been seriously shakened. The only possible way to ever overcome deeply embedded destruction is to pursue restoration as only the Master delivers. My rage to survive grew day by day until it reached a level that both God and man knew I was serious about. It did not matter if I were laughed at, ridiculed, or talked about. All that mattered to me was that I would know, live in, sleep in, and embrace restoration totally.

I once heard a missionary make a notable statement about her third-world travels. She declared that after returning to the States she had to force out of her mind some conditions of suffering that she had seen, if she were to live healthy from day to day. Some conditions of human life that existed there were so deplorable that, if she allowed the mental photos to continue, they would rob her of her own ability to live day to day. She had to resolve that what she could contribute in God's own way of using her life was being done and leave all else to God. Carrying the pains of what she knew would not fix the problem.

We too, as God's people, must let go. If we ever want to be able to live healthy lives, spiritually and in general, we must let go. You may ask, let go of what? Letting go of what is behind, as Paul stated, is the only way to truly move towards the prize. (See Philippians 3:13.) Let's park here for a moment. The desire or rage to survive shows itself many times in this fashion. We want to forget all the harmful things we have ever experienced. Many times we try and fail, just as I did for a while. Then one night I asked God to show me how to truly forget anything and everything that was ever done to me. I asked God to satisfy this inner drive in me to survive such devastation. I was sincere in my asking, meaning that if God made it plain I would do it. I just needed something on my level that would show me how to forget the things that needed to be eliminated from my mind. Paul states:

> Brethren, I do not count myself to have apprehended; but one thing I do, forgetting those things which are behind and reaching forward to those things which are ahead, I press toward the goal for the prize of the upward

call of God in Christ Jesus. Therefore let us, as many as are mature, have this mind; and if in anything you think otherwise, God will reveal even this to you.
—Phillippians 3:13–15

Again, we all try to put things behind us at times so the reason we don't succeed is not because we don't want to. It is because we don't know how to. At least that was what happened in my case. I would have welcomed the sweetness of freedom from mental torture, but how? Here is what the Word of the Lord gave me when I sought for this hidden meaning. God told me to picture the plant at my door, which I pass each day as I come and go. God said do not water that plant and what do you get? Do not give that plant any nourishment. Walk past that plant, although it is there, and give it nothing: no water, no food, and no attention. To neglect that plant is equivalent to forgetting that plant. Neglect it and give it nothing. Paul is telling us in the Word of God to never water or nourish the bad, the evil, or the unfortunate things that have happened to us. Let the plant die. Give it nothing. When a thought comes to your mind don't feed it, and resist feeding it. James 4:7 states, "Resist the devil and he will flee from you." Don't water anything that is not from God. Just as a neglected plant will die, those bad things from your past will die too. In fact, they can become so dead that you will not know what others are talking about at times.

However, this would be surviving, and the enemy of our souls is always there to try to make us nourish the bad thoughts and experiences from the past. In our thoughts we tend to hang around what he, she, and they did to us. We water those things and they grow bigger and bigger. Many times they are more monstrous now than when they actually happened. This is because we nourished them and fed them. Only respond to the desire within you to survive. Only water what will propel you toward what lies ahead. If it is not part of the press to get you on to the prize of the upward call of God then don't pamper, nourish, and think on it in any way.

In order to answer the rage to survive that we have we must neglect, forget, and deliberately skip our appointment with misery and our conversation with Ms. She- and He-sure-did-do-all-those-things-to-me. Tell those things that nobody's home. Don't answer the knock at the door that says, *I want to come in and sit awhile and discuss all those horrible things life has done to you.* Tell the enemy that you have an appointment with Restoration, and he is not invited. Keep that appointment with Restoration by only nourishing the things that will help you get there. One day you will answer the knock at the door and say, *Hello, RESTORATION, I have been expecting you.* You will say to RESTORATION, *This is why I sent a spiritual telegram proclaiming that there is a rage and a desire in me that will not quit until I walk in liberty and freedom and I can taste reform for myself.* Come and get it because it is yours. When you finish this book your thirst for divine survival will be quenched. Not because you have it all, but because you will know what you need to do.

Now, somewhere about eighteen to twenty years into my marriage, life had really beaten me up bad. I mean real bad, and I had helped the process with my poor decisions. If it was so bad, why did I stay for more than ten years? Good question, isn't it? I did nothing to stop it or turn it off except what I did best: I fought with every breath in me to not let things get the best of me. It was important to me to never let anyone say that anything got to me. I wanted to be known for how well I could survive life's strange darts. I hated losing at anything. I did not associate myself with losers. The only thing I ever did with losers was try to provoke them to become winners.

People who lost at life's battles were weak to me, so I set out to prove my strengths. I recall a sister in the church coming to me once after a service saying, "If you would just go ahead and cry we would understand you better. In fact, we expect you to cry about all this." It was as if she was saying that the evidence of my storm would be my tears. The folks around me needed to see me fold, cry, or break. That would confirm how human I was. The statement made me angry enough to make a firm commitment to never allow them to see me cry or break. I succeeded. For twenty or so years at that church I would not shed one tear for people to see. While many testified in tears about their critical needs during prayer requests, I would not. For years every time I stood to speak I would only talk of how all my blessings outweighed my troubles. My list of blessings made my list of problems seem small but for a moment.

Most of my time, however, was spent trying to figure out how to get through the evening without passing out. My emotions were becoming very frail, but then I would think about how I couldn't let the devil win. I would cling to God as if my life depended on it, because it did. During the stormy seas of life I had to make many wise choices. As I look back on things now those choices made me what I am today. There were opportunities, among gentlemen acquaintances of mine, for me to run off from it all. I could get away from the abuse and start over with someone else who cared. I wanted to take on the offers; that is, my flesh did. I wanted to show him a thing or two. But my rage to survive was so strong that many times after a long look at things I knew that I had to do it under the right terms. I just was not there yet. I would look at my four children and say, *I can't do it to them.*

My inner drive to survive grew and I applied myself at first, before all the stupid thoughts to give up on God, to sensible activities. I attended church services at least four or five times a week for years. The other days I spent at my favorite coffee shops and in the malls pretending that nothing was wrong. My career helped a lot because God had made me very successful. I remember coming into work one day as professional as I could be and something unexpected happened. I walked into the chief financial officer's office that day and just broke into tears. I had no notice. Nothing warned me that this would happen. I had been up all night struggling with the scenes of every encounter I had made of all the betrayals. I was weak emotionally and physically. I had gotten everyone off to school. I think it was one of those days when I had to pull my car over to the side of the road because I could not see the road for my tears. I would play a song over and over again in my mind until finally I arrived at work. I was not aware that my system was on overload.

I was the bionic woman. You know, bionic! Can't-get-me-down person. To my surprise, survival can still feel pain. Survival, though a good thing, cannot erase the nightmare. The will to survive does not take you from the storm; it gets you through it by the grace of God. The Scriptures say that "if [we] faint in the day of adversity, [our] strength is small" (Prov. 24:10). I had to survive. I refused to be called small. Call me a lot of things, but don't call me weak. Don't call me small. How foolish I was. All that will and strength could have been used in a more productive way. All I cared about was not letting the other person know they beat me. This was sort of like a careless builder who builds a house so fast and so wreckless, not caring how he is putting the house together. When I finished putting things together with all that surviving will, the house

I had was a house of horror. No one could live in it. No one wanted it anymore. The children begged me to leave. I was doing all the wrong kind of surviving. Listening and obeying God's voice is true survival. I missed this part at first. I could not hear the Holy Spirit's direction because I had a distorted view of what I needed to do.

God wanted me to recognize who He said I was. God wanted me to stand on His Word and live in peace as He would direct, but my mind was all clouded up with proving points. The fight was truly on and nothing would take me out. The devil was on his mission to kill, steal, and destroy. (See John 10:10.) He wanted to kill me and any chance for an abundant life, steal all my dreams, and destroy any possible hope at all. He truly almost succeeded. I aided him in this assignment because of ignorance. Let me explain. I got saved under the old teaching that bad things came from God because He wanted to teach me something. If God was teaching me something, it sure did not make much sense to pray to Him to get me out of my mess, now did it?

I was told for many years that God did not want me to leave my husband. He wanted me to stay in my test. The truth is God wanted me to know Him in His fullness. He did not order this for me. No two situations are alike and that is why we must learn to live close enough to God to seek Him for direction and to hear His voice for ourselves. The directions given me will not work for you, because God answered *me*. Mine are not necessarily applicable to what you are faced with. Ask God how to launch into the abundant living explained in His Word. He is obligated to tell you. The Bible tells us that if any man "lacks wisdom, let him ask of God, who gives to all liberally and without reproach, and it will be given to him" (James 1:5). So God must be true to His

Word and He cannot lie, so ask Him. Look for an answer and seek with your whole heart and you will find Him. If you do not find Him, then either He lied or you lied that you truly sought. I say "let God be true but every man a liar" (Rom. 3:4). We will find Him when we have sought as the Word of God explains. God never abuses His children nor does He give anyone else permission to do so. However, if you are not sure of this you will consent to the wrong things in your life. Does it sound like God to you that He would want His children to be abused and tormented in life?

Here is what you do if you find yourself in a mess that God did not call you to. Never do something just because someone else does it. Live close to God in order to hear how the Spirit is directing you. Many times God's direction does not direct you out of the mess, but He directs you how to get through it. When you see God's way through your specific situations, then and only then are you ready for real instructions. During the times we scream, kick, and act like a fool we would cause more problems to attempt to run out into a world that is ready to eat you alive. When King David was distressed and at his wits' end after the Amalekites had taken all his stuff, he inquired of the Lord if he should pursue and go reclaim what was taken from him. God instructed David to pursue for "you shall surely overtake them and without fail recover all" (1 Sam. 30.) Go get your stuff back, man or woman of God. Your stuff is all that God wants you to have pertaining to a godly life. Go get it and God will be with you as He has promised in His Word to never leave us or forsake us. He spoke to Joshua with these words when giving him instructions, "I will not leave you nor forsake you" (Josh. 1:5). However, we are to make sure that our instructions come from God as Joshua did. We can only get those instructions by living so that we can discern His voice. Take hold of peace, emotions, mental stability, and clarity about who you are. Live like the kings and queens we are and cease living as slaves to this world's ungodly reign.

Getting your stuff back just simply means reclaiming the good life. Jesus talks about it. He said His yoke is easy and His burden light, and you shall find rest unto your souls (Matt. 11:29–30). I have my stuff back and am enjoying it so much that I want you too to taste what it is like. I am where my Father wants me to be: "My beloved is mine, and I am his" (Song of Sol. 2:16). Too many times we don't allow our Beloved (God) to love us, and we just say in mere words that I am His. If your Beloved (God) is truly all that and more, then allow Him to show you who He is. Jesus said, "Fear not, little [children]; for it is your Father's good pleasure to give you the kingdom" (Luke 12:32, KJV). Let God do what He gets good pleasure from. He gets good pleasure from giving you the kingdom. What is in the kingdom? Abundant living is in the kingdom, more than you can ask or think. What eye has not seen nor ear heard—all these are in the kingdom and more (1 Cor. 2:9).

Chapter 3

All Storms Are Transitory

Many natural storms are caused by a combination of adverse conditions that do not mix calmly together. Instead, when certain ripe weather components meet, a storm emerges. Life is very similar to this in some ways. When certain adverse, uncooperative conditions merge together a storm ensues. When we allow mixtures of messes into our lives, little by little the gathering of what will become an unbearable storm surfaces. I am not blaming us for the storms that come. We all know that the enemy of our souls comes to kill, steal, and destroy (John 10:10). Storms kill; storms steal and destroy in the natural and in the spiritual also.

I provided the wrong conditions for the storms in my life to grow in strength more and more until they heightened to incomprehensible levels. But I learned something very valuable during this time. I learned that there is a place in the eye of the storm that is very calm. While all around me the storm was raging, I learned how to trust my way right out of the turmoil. I learned later than I would have liked to; but the fact, is I did learn. I learned how to allow God to be God. All storms are transitory. It does not matter how fierce the severity or how small the storm—no storm can last forever. I must tell you again: all storms are transitory! Then why do our storms as children of God seem to last forever? They last so long because we do not take our way of escape. God makes the way for our escape, but it is up to us to take it. We do not take it because we don't see it or we don't know it is our escape.

We must get to high ground in order to see the plan of escape designed by God. Let me explain. One night I was asleep and a dream came to me that I was somehow caught in a tunnel of some sort. This tunnel had so many different levels and angles. Well, all of a sudden there was an urgency to run for safety because the turbulent storms seemed to worsen, and the probability of surviving appeared weak. I lay asleep and heard a voice directing me, saying, "Get to higher ground." So I did. I ran with all my might to higher ground, and when I got way up higher I saw something that amazed me. I saw an open door that I had not seen before. I launched toward that open door and all the peace, safety, and tranquility that it had on the other side. Then I awoke thinking: *Now what was that all about?*

Just now, as I was pondering that dream, the Spirit of the Lord visited me and said to tell the readers to get to higher ground in order to see the way of escape. You can't see what He has for you in the plains. Battles are lost in the plains and in the valleys, where your enemy has the advantage. Your observation is different when on the high ground. In war, when men are ambushed as they go through valleys or low grounds, the attack, even when short in duration, seems to last forever. Being caught on low ground is no help at all. Get to the high ground so you can observe better and see the plans of escape. Paul to the Philippians said, "That I may know Him and the power of His resurrection" (Phil. 3:10). You will never truly know the power of who He is from the low ground. To know Him you must go to the high ground. That's where you hear Him say, "Peace, be still." Jesus has spoken many times for us to have abundant life, but when we stay on the low ground of life we cannot hear Him and the instructions for us. He is not down in the low ground. Remember, He has risen from the dead and He is Lord. You should rise also from the stormy seas and hear God's deliverance and observe His plan of escape.

Always know that plans of escape don't necessarily mean leaving in the physical. Don't think you must pack bags and run off to some unknown territory. God is a purposeful God. He is a wise God. He is faithful and "will not allow you to be tempted beyond what you are able, but with the temptation will also make the way of escape" (1 Cor. 10:13). However, if you abide in the lowlands you will not see His plans for you. When you get way up high, the storms can't destroy you there. The storms can't touch you there. Our storms seem to last forever because we never move from its damage, its destructive result. We live, day in and day out, in the storm's aftermath. Many times we will not allow the storm to die. Any storm will eventually weaken and go into a miniscule state, given the right setting in which to do so. Let me explain. A hurricane rising in the northern Atlantic has great speed, but meteorologists forecast that if the storm travels southward it will drop in speed due to the climate of that region. However, meteorologists also know that further east, or other directions, the conditions are ripe to produce an even fiercer storm. This is what many of us do at times and what I also did for awhile: we don't take our minds and emotions and strengths to where we can weaken the storm that is raging. We go up on the radar into the territory that will only make the storm fiercer and give it longevity to go on and on.

We must also allow the storm to end. It will transition right out of our lives given the proper ground to do so. Maybe some of you did something stupid, the way I did in a certain period of my life. Somewhere around my twenty-third year of marriage, I had had all I could take. I could not survive a moment longer in the turmoil and situation at hand. Now your situation may or may not be the same, but this will help you anyway. I managed through a lot of difficult processes to get the house to the children and myself by using our justice system. You can't just threaten people, so I did something about it. After the authorities were involved I finally felt like I could get some rest from my stormy lifestyle. I had gone before a judge one afternoon and heard him explain just how serious my situation was.

I just needed to feel like a person again. I thought I was ready to move on in life and start over, and I was for a little while. I was not on high ground with the Lord because I was confused and I knew that God knew it too. I was just worn out. I felt like I had no physical, mental, or spiritual life left.

I went to the State Attorney's office in the town where I live. A restraining order was issued and for the first time in many years I felt peaceful. I had a good job so I could take care of myself. In fact, I had the better job of the two. Was the situation really over? Next stop: total freedom, right? Wrong! Six months later and even with children and family begging me, I allowed the storm back into my life by allowing his return. How stupid was this decision for me? Real dumb! I even called my attorney and withdrew the divorce proceedings. I spent so much time trying to change the other person instead of working on the things that needed changing about me. The next few years were a nightmare, and I deserved it. I had gone into hostile territory with my eyes wide open. If ever I needed God, I needed Him now. This was when people began to make plans to have me committed to an institution. Not because of what I had done, but because of what was being done to me. They knew I could never survive it. But "thanks be unto God, which always causeth us to triumph" (2 Cor. 2:14, KJV). "This is the victory that overcometh the world, even our faith" (1 John 5:4, KJV). That is all I had by the time the devil had drained every ounce of life, peace, and joy from me. I looked to my faith in God to pull me out of this mess and He did.

Destiny was so wrapped up in my loins that even with the bitter evils I was experiencing nothing could keep me from finding high ground in God. I needed God now more than ever before. I can say, as the psalmist David said, that His "lovingkindness is better than life" (Ps. 63:3, KJV). Philippians 1:12 came alive in my life. It reads: "But I want you to know, brethren, that the things which happened to me have actually turned out for the furtherance of the gospel." In Ephesians, Paul says, "Do not be unwise, but understand what the will of the Lord is" (Eph. 5:17). Many times storms don't seem to end because we do not understand what the will of the Lord is. We should walk in wisdom. The next time God gave me a way of escape I took it and never looked back. I will tell you of that plan of escape in a later chapter. Another reason we should allow God to show us how to let the storm end is because the sooner we do, we can get down to the real work. The real work is restoring the land that the storm has so unmercifully destroyed. You know how it is. After a hurricane here in the United States we hear reports of the storm's destruction estimated in dollar value. It is stated over and over that to rebuild this or that region will cost, sometimes, into the billions of dollars. That is when the real work begins. You can never get down to business if you don't allow the storm to transition right out of your life. You will look back one day and ask: *How did I ever allow something so small to bother me? What was I thinking about?* It is not because the storm was really insignificant, but because moving on from it makes it difficult to even remember the storm's initial rage. We can indeed go so far past the storm that it takes effort to recall we even had such a battle with life.

At twenty-nine years of marriage the one thing I found out is that no storm can last forever. Even the fiercest storm will die out at some point and become something of the past. You can allow a storm to stay with you longer than intended or you can choose the high road and have faith in God. Obedience and faith are very important to your spiritual survival.

Let's look at the children of Israel. They walked in disobedience and experienced storm after storm. You cannot live in conditions unfavorable to God and have His perfect peace. In Deuteronomy, God told His people not to plant any tree "as a wooden image" or set up sacred pillars. (See Deuteronomy 16:21–22.) Doing so brought turmoil into their lives because righteousness cannot fellowship with evil. We have other types of things we worship that God gets no glory from. When a storm arises we say, *Why did God let this happen?* Actually, I let the storm almost destroy me. I allowed the storm to rob me of the peace that God intended. I do believe that when we listen to the voice of God—not the voice of all our friends—He will deliver us in His way from every ungodly stronghold. You only find this by walking close to Him. You can't hear your instructions unless you are close enough to Him to hear the soft, still voice as it speaks. Many times the storms of life have really ended, but we bring them back to life; we resurrect them and make our abode with them so it seems like they did not end. Your storm too will end if you allow it to.

When the storm finally ended for me and the scales fell from my eyes I was in such bad shape that neither the Salvation Army, all of America's charities, missionaries from faraway lands, Big Brothers, Big Sisters, nor Moses, Paul, Peter or John would have tackled the task to rebuild me again. I was a destructive mess! Only God would tackle this tremendous job to rebuild a person demolished and devastated to this degree. Most of my issues and problems were from what I was doing to myself. But thanks be unto God who giveth us the victory (2 Cor. 2:14). "This is the victory that overcometh the world, even our faith" (1 John 5:4, KJV). Keep in mind, as we start our restoration journey, that faith is belief in action. Belief that is resting is hope. Hope wants some help. Faith is the help. The Bible in fact tells us this. "Faith is the substance of things hoped for" (Heb. 11:1, KJV). The sureness of the things hoped for is faith. Sureness is what guarantees things. Faith is the guarantee of your hopes.

Let me go deeper. Walk with me in this. "Faith is the substance of things hoped for" (Heb. 11:1, KJV). If you hope for a chocolate cake then you had better use the substance that guarantees a chocolate cake. What is the substance of a chocolate cake? CHOCOLATE, now isn't it? Let me prove it. You may burn your chocolate cake, but you still have a chocolate cake. You don't have a burnt lemon cake because chocolate was your substance. You see, eggs, butter, and flour are in all cakes. These are your general ingredients. To ensure a chocolate cake, you must use the substance of what is hoped for. Well, now faith is the substance of the things we hope for. If you want abundant life you had better make sure faith is in the batter. All that other stuff, good singing, a shout now and then, and the other is just fine, but if the faith is not there—if your real substance or the sureness of faith is not there—you will not get the things hoped for. So if you want a chocolate cake you had better use some kind of chocolate as your sureness. If you want the things hoped for in your life, you had better put FAITH in the batter. Faith is the only instrument that can see further than what has been produced for the temporary time in this realm of the natural.

Chocolate is the only thing that can give you a chocolate cake. No chocolate, no chocolate cake. You may still have a cake, but it will not be chocolate. No faith, no things hoped for produced by God. You may get some things in life but you will not get what only faith produces. Since no storm is going to last forever, why not start now believing God for the best future yet? Some people say it, sing it, or doubt it, but the best is truly yet to come. I am embracing it every day of my life. I took God at His Word and it is not that I have obtained all nor have I seized all, but I have my mind on the upward prize of the call of Christ Jesus. You can't press toward the upward call and live in the downward call at the same time. I love what the psalmist David spoke when he said:

> Lift up your heads, O ye gates; and be ye lifted up, ye everlasting doors; and the King of glory shall come in. Who is this King of glory? The LORD strong and mighty, the LORD mighty in battle.
>
> —PSALM 24:7–8, KJV

Lift up your heads; the battle is over; the storm is past, but only if you let go of it. Listen to God's voice and He will direct you through your Red Sea, and the Egyptians you see today (things chasing you) you will see no more forever (Exod. 14:13). Hide yourself in God while the storm passes by. And Jesus said, "Peace, be still" (Mark 4:39).

Chapter 4

Step 1: Root Out

As we go into Step One of restoration, keep in mind the story about the fig tree that Jesus cursed because it had no fruit on it. (See Matthew 21:19–21.) The fig tree was dried up from the root. It was not the areas of what you could see that was killed. The tree was killed at the root, the area not immediately visible to the eye. The killing or cursing of the root, or core of the tree, is what caused it to cease from bearing fruit. So as we talk more on "Step 1: Root Out," keep in mind the destruction of where the strength or substance being destroyed actually results in the destruction of the intended fruit or the product coming from the roots.

We are finally here, in the precious halls of restoration. I hope you did not skip ahead because the previous chapters are very important in order that you have all the right pieces as we launch into step one of restoration. It took awhile, but you had to understand the horribly bad shape I was in. You needed to know that I had degenerated into such a worthless state that only God wanted this project! Thirty years in captivity is a very long time. If I had been God, I would not have taken me on. You are unable to wrap your mind around how worthless my life seemed to me. But there were treasures of discoveries just waiting for me to unveil.

Our divine formula for total restoration is found in Jeremiah's directives from God. I need you to understand that Jeremiah was not a prophet who brought a message of repentance and surrender only in order to receive from God. Jeremiah's message was not that of just driving God's people from their backslidden and false worship back to God, initially. Jeremiah's job was to first announce the sure doom of captivity along with bringing awareness to the condition God's people were in. In the beginning, Jeremiah had to tell them that Babel's control was a sure thing. (See Jeremiah 1:14–15.)

Isaiah's job was to turn the people from false worship and from the evil of their doings back to God. Isaiah tried to stir their conscience to the Maker, their Redeemer and the only one and true God. When Isaiah failed at total reformation of the people of God there was only one consequence. That consequence was to live in the world without their God providing and protecting them. So after forty years of prophetic words from the prophet Isaiah we now move into another phase.

Let us pause here to see how this relates to us today. Based on the Scriptures, many times our worship is not true worship. We worship everything but the One True God. We set up false gods. Often, we have nothing but religion and we want God to accept it. Neither my worship nor my life was where it should have been. If it had been I would not have ended up in thirty years of captivity. God's people had seventy years of Babylonian control to endure because of their own misgivings. (See Jeremiah 25:11; 29:10; Daniel 9:2.) God does not send evil into our lives; we bring it on by our decisions. Our decisions drive our circumstances. This may be a little hard to understand, but God did not leave the children of Israel;

they left Him. This resulted in Him not being around when needed. Their decisions of evil, false worship dictated the circumstances they woke up to. God is not the god of evil captivity. The soon captivity and Babel bondage of God's people was revealed to Jeremiah before it happened. Jeremiah saw what was going to break forth. (See Jeremiah 1:12–14.) God knew that when His people's captivity ended they would not just all of a sudden be OK.

Jeremiah had a difficult job in that he prophetically saw the captivity, the endured sufferings, and also the total restoration plan for God's people. God gave Jeremiah the formula. This formula will work no matter what situation you have in life. It does not matter what ungodly, unmentionable, hellish bondage you find yourself in. Before you were even born God gave Jeremiah the solution and formula for reformation. I needed this formula because life was closing in on me fast. I lacked so much understanding about life and how all this had happened to me. They were in bondage, but the end of the seventy years was in sight and God knew they needed a special message if they were to survive what had happened to them. So while yet in captivity He told Jeremiah to tell them that He had some good plans for them:

> For I know the thoughts that I think toward you, saith the LORD, thoughts of peace, and not of evil, to give you an expected end.
> —JEREMIAH 29:11, KJV

In order to see this good plan there had to be something done on their part. Let's look at their part, or our part today. Jeremiah 29:13 states, "You will seek Me and find Me, when you search for Me with all your heart." Verse 11 gives the end result: He will "give you a future and a hope." Verse 13 tells how a future and a hope start. Now the reason the end result of our seeking with a whole heart is given first is because God declares the end from the beginning, according to the prophet Isaiah. (See Isaiah 46:10.) This is why in the first chapter of Jeremiah God gave the formula at the beginning to be used for His plan of restoration. Many people have plans for reformation but I would rather "let God be true but every man a liar" (Rom. 3:4). God knows what got us in these conditions and only God can reveal and accomplish how to get us out.

Captivity and bondage rob us of many vital lifelong desires and fulfillment. God revealed to Jeremiah how to bring His people back to where they needed to be. (See Jeremiah 1:10.) The first step in our journey to completeness is to "ROOT OUT." This instruction was given first because I believe the order is essential. No matter what has been done against us in life the negative effect or the damage and abuse lurking that tend to show their heads whenever they want to must be rooted out. Many say, *I have overcome what was done to me,* but unless the core or the root of what caused your condition is dealt with, it is just a matter of time before the root of your problems will revisit you again. God knew that His people had to have a lot of Babylonian stuff rooted out of them. They had been stubborn and disobedient, and the core had to go. The reason we never grow and don't go on and develop properly is because the root of things is still there. A weed that is only broken off above ground will always sprout up again because the root is still there. We don't deal with the problems inside of us; we keep with it and in some cases those ugly strong roots get bigger and bigger. God had a lot for His people, but He also knew that unless the root of what made them the way they were was gone they would never embrace the fullness of the kingdom.

Let me explain further about rooting something out. When something is rooted it is firmly planted or established. In order to even begin our journey to restoration the roots of what caused our distress many times lie planted in us so deep they have become a part of who we are. When God told Jeremiah to root out He was talking about the underground part of what is planted. When something is rooted out of us it is no longer a part of us. We don't carry around what is out of us. Becoming whole again after misuse of any kind requires the rooting up or going deep into the heart of the matter and bringing the core out. Things that come against you will not prevail or win if the rooting out of what would otherwise overthrow us has occurred.

There was so much mess rooted inside of me. Things related to why I chose such a person for my life, why I stayed in the horror, why I operated in gross blindness. Pride, pretense, and not wanting to become a certain statistic all had roots that combined forces and became strongholds in my life. My father was a drunkard and so the pain from not having fatherly love drove me to pretend there was love in a loveless situation. The good planting cannot occur unless the rooting out of the bad happens. Or the things that spring up from bad roots will eventually choke out the good things. The good roots are overpowered by all the rotten roots to the degree that the land looks corrupt and unattractive. Take the root of your problems or the core of your grief and spiritually hold it out in front of you. Turn it over, look over it, and say to God: *This root is too big for me to handle. It is imbedded so far down in me that when I merely tug on it, I feel pain. When I try to wiggle loose from these roots the pain is unbearable.*

God wants us "rooted and built up in Him and established in the faith" (Col. 2:7). God spoke of the plans in Jeremiah 29:11:

"For I know the thoughts that I think toward you, says the Lord, thoughts of peace and not of evil to give you a future and a hope." We need to understand when and why these words were given. Jeremiah's prophetic revelation showed him that Israel would be loosed after certain years and that they needed to know there are good plans in view for them. Let's go back to the construction site example. When builders decide that they would like to build in certain areas, before the actual building or home is placed, the land must be prepared in order to properly build upon it. One of the things I have always seen is they go in and take out a lot of stuff, junk, garbage, dirt, glass, and all sorts of useless materials taking up the space where they desire to build something beautiful. Many times they even bring in a dumpster to haul all that useless stuff off. They go way, way into the ground taking away dirt from down deep in order to make way for the foundation. God's direction to Jeremiah for the people was to root out because God was coming through with what He wanted to build. We need to let go of all the junk that hurt us way down on the inside. Whether it be betrayal, physical or emotional abuse, disappointments, or shattered dreams, the scars must be rooted out. These things must be placed into our spiritual dumpsters if we are ever to be restored.

Holding on to the bitter pills that came our way in life is like not having control of where you go in life. While you are holding things they are also holding you as well. When you let go of them, in turn they let go of you. You have to stay there with the bad in order for it to have you. It takes effort as it did for me to root out the undesirable things in our lives. Unless we let go of people who caused us pain and destroy their ungodly powers we will wander in pity and unfulfilled visions. In fact, why give anything or anyone that much power over you? This is a lot of what made me do certain things. Before I learned how to allow God to do all for me, I made sure I never let him, her, them, or it have the better of me. God placed a determination within me to have God prove to me that He is everything His Word says He is.

That longing was misplaced many times in that I used it the wrong way. I would have seen just who God really was in my life had I allowed Him sooner to take care of me. However, later in life when I did step out on the faith of the Word, He could prove it more because I was operating on just faith alone. I had nothing else to lean on. I was stripped of everything except the turmoil that I always felt brewing inside of me from the misuse I had just stepped away from. I felt all of the things that needed to be rooted out of me. I just did not know how it would ever happen. I wanted so badly to walk in peace and joy with freedom to love and be loved. I was suffering badly with the scars from the years past. What I felt and who I was did not make sense. I had always been a fun-loving, happy person; one that was full of life. Now I found myself using night hours to cry about where I was, alone and sad. Then one day I made a spiritual list of all the things I truly wanted in my life that I felt would indeed bring happiness.

I came to a shocking revelation. I was not on the road that leads to those good things. Oh, I am not talking about just being saved. That road was fine. I knew the Lord. You can know the Lord and still let life pin you down in pity, disgust, shame, and pain. Why live for the Lord, barely getting by? I realized that I did not want to spend my life as a just-get-by person. So what he lived without regard for me all those years? So what the painful, hellish family life I experienced? Why let who he was dictate who I should be or how I should live? Why should I not enjoy the blessings of God and walk right into the tremendous abundance only found in being restored? How are you going to build beauty on top of pain, grief, worry, and disdain? Who said I was supposed to allow another's deficiencies affect my efficiencies? Sounds good, but I did not know how to make it happen on my own.

Sometimes our pain and abuse go so deep that we can't put it into words, much less try to triumph over the pain. This takes the Master's involvement. Only the Master can root out from the root and make the vessel as it should have been all along. It was too great a job for me, and it is too great for you. We have a part, but not the part we think. In the rooting out process it is our job to be flexible with the Holy Spirit. Let me explain. It is revealed how messed up we are, and we are truly at times messed up. Just look at it. We did not sleep last night because of what someone did to us. We cry during day hours and we have pity parties all our own. We are just messed up because someone did something to us. As I look back on life, I said this long ago, that if I had known then what I know now I would have slipped someone a little payoff money to keep my husband from coming back. You never know how good something tastes until you taste it. When I got ready to get my divorce, things had been so plucked out by the root that as he struggled and deliberately tried to delay and stop it, I offered to pay his plane fare, limo fare, and everything else just to get him into the court room quickly for my divorce. The day my final papers arrived I danced like David. (See 2 Samuel 6:14.)

God never designed it for me to live as I had lived all those years. I finally tasted what it was like to know peace of heart, worth the Bible's way, and joy so unspeakable it made me quiver. The trees looked better, the sky was different; I was now embracing what my Father thought of me and it felt good, good, good. I remember a phone call I received from my daughter while things were being rooted out of me. I told someone it felt like a surgical operation going deep into my organs without any anesthesia being used. You know that is painful. When the stuff that should not be there is being rooted out it just plain old HURTS! Tell the truth—it hurts so badly. But one day that surgical procedure is over and the root is out and we can start anew.

In our society today the correctional systems are failing to a large degree. We are building more prisons than ever in history and still bursting at the seams. The numbers of inmates who are repeat offenders are growing in staggering proportions. Until we pry the infected areas open, dig out the bacteria, and dig out the root of the defect the vicious cycle will continue. The root of the infection must be removed in order to effectively build again. This is why the first step is "Root Out." We cannot successfully build until the rooting out occurs. Men and women are loosed today, and so were the children of Israel loosed. But God knew that being loosed and being fully restored are very different. Reformation is the corrective process applied to the defective. To make better by the removal of the faulted area is true reform. Reform by any other method is called a bandage application. This application is only temporary and can provide no permanent reform. God knew this and so He directed Jeremiah to root out. This is the only way to do it. Root it out! All the way out! Allow God to remove all the faults that should not be there; all the faulted areas that have made us weak unbelievers.

There is absolutely nothing that can be withheld from us if we do it by God's method. Remember He told Jeremiah that He had all these good plans and hope of a good future after the instructions on rooting out the things that did not belong. I did it and you can too. I experienced a very painful time when

I made a firm commitment to remove, by God's help, each root of bitterness that showed its evil head. I allowed matters and issues to die from the root giving them no ground to grow on and God blessed me for it. He blessed everything I attempted to do because I said, like Peter did, "Lord, not my feet only, but also my hands and my head!" (John 13:9).

A dentist, when preparing a root canal treatment, must first clean out all debris, bacteria, and even the nerve root in order to treat the problem. Have you ever seen how small the nerve root on the tooth is that causes so much pain? It is very small, yet if not removed fully it will surface again and again. The pain will come back and the situation will come back too, unless you get rid of the roots. Only when the area is clean and free of defective roots does the dentist safely fill it with new substance and seal it to be sure of no more disturbances. God wants to remove the root causing the problems and fill us with His Holy Spirit. We can then say, as Paul said to the Corinthians, it is God "who establishes us with you in Christ and has anointed us is God, who also has sealed us and given us the Spirit in our hearts as a guarantee" (2 Cor. 1:21–22).

Will the Church, people of God, ever truly deal with the root of our failures such as hatred, abandonment, racism, ungratefulness, unkindness, self-seeking, money loving, pride, callous hearts, and love for everything other than what our country was supposed to be built upon? We say, "In God we trust." Why not trust when He shows us the error of our own times and ways by rooting out for a better you and me? The rooting out process will remedy any situation. The Word speaks of laying the ax to the root. (See Matthew 3:10.) Something that has no root will eventually wither away. No root, no production. The weaknesses and destructive behavior in our lives should be treated like the instructions given for the sycamine tree or the mulberry tree. Pluck them up from the roots and cast them into the sea. (See Luke 17:6, KJV and NKJV.) "Looking carefully lest anyone fall short of the grace of God; lest any root of bitterness springing up cause trouble" (Heb. 12:15). We must get rid of the things inside us at the root if we are ever to live a life that displays the power of God bestowed upon us. Don't allow your past, your present circumstances, or what you fear to come keep you from experiencing God's best.

Chapter 5

Step 2: Pull Down

I N THIS CHAPTER we will talk about how to demolish some things that God shows us should not be part of our character or part of our behavior. These are strongholds. We will discuss how to pull down those things that need to be pulled down from our hearts and lives. Strongholds have to go if you want to succeed on your restoration journey. Many strongholds are the result of another type of action, such as living in shame from what someone else did to us. Abuse, abandonment, and betrayals weaken us and produce shame many times. Shame inflicts a loss of dignity upon us. In fact, it is the loss of dignity and shame that may cause many wrong or improper follow-up decisions. We are trying to cover the shame instead of dealing with the issue.

Never conceal or deny what needs to be pulled down from the place in your life, heart, and emotions that are not part of a godly life. Never store the shame; deal with the issues that created the shame. By doing so the shame has to leave because your ability to deal with issues gives it no place to lurk in your life. People who shame themselves into certain actions many times just go on to commit more and more shameful actions.

Why not get rid of the shameful ways and look to the double everlasting joy we have been promised? (See Isaiah 61:7.) You can never receive the double if you don't cease to behave in the ways that weakness and self-pity make us. If you are still walking around mourning your losses, then you have not made the trade. If you have mourned then you have a promise that beauty will come and replace the ashes of what you are dealing with. (See Isaiah 61:3.) The beauty can't take over because we don't let go of the ashes. Both of them can't abide at the same time.

This can even apply to many different situations and challenges as you walk in this life. Strongholds must be demolished. Don't play with them. Don't allow them to hang out. You know what they are in your life. I don't. I do know that in a weakened unrestored state they lurk and help the bondage to continue and, many times, grow deeper. Once they are discovered, ask the Master for the will to take them out. Paul said it this way, "For the weapons of our warfare are not carnal but mighty in God for pulling down strongholds" (2 Cor. 10:4). Oops, there it is. Pull that stuff down. I will tell you how I did it.

I made an amazing discovery. It may not be amazing to you, but it was to me. For years I thought that strongholds were the things that had me bound. Saying things like: *I never do this; I can't turn my life around; I have not worked in years; I must stay in the abuse because he and I have never worked on the relationship; although he or she sleeps around, this is the reason I am staying.* The thing that makes these strongholds come to life is your mindset. The natural or personal things are not the stronghold, but it is how you think that creates the stronghold. Have you ever heard someone say, "You know he stays with her even though he knows she sleeps around on him"? She, the person, is not his stronghold. The way he thinks is the stronghold. Remember, as "he thinketh in his heart, so is he" (Prov. 23:7, KJV).

Strongholds are fortresses that we build with our thoughts, laying one brick (one excuse) at a time. We keep building and building with these thoughts until the power of the stronghold becomes how we eat, think, work, sit, and play. It is a part of us. If you are willing to pull down your strongholds God will do it for you; you just provide the faith in Him that He is doing what is best for His children. Think of a beautiful, high fortress that guards what is inside the building it was erected to protect. This is where I was in life. During those many years of self-inflicted bondage I had such a beautiful, towering stronghold constructed by my thought processes.

To prove it was a stronghold constructed by my thought processes I will share the following. The person, the houses, everything I had before, which I thought I did not want to lose, was still there when I left. What changed? My thought process changed. I wanted what Jesus said in His Word: "Fear not, little [children]; for it is your Father's good pleasure to give you the kingdom". (Luke 12:32, KJV). Since it was God's good pleasure to give me the kingdom, I thought differently and said, *Why not allow God to have some pleasures?* He gets pleasure from giving me the kingdom. So it doesn't make sense for me to keep God from doing what He gets pleasure from. What is in the kingdom? Peace, joy, and abundant living, based on what my Bible tells me. I was helping the devil so the things God wanted to get pleasure out of giving to me could not break through because of the fortress or strongholds keeping them out.

If you will tear down, demolish, and pull down all the things that have you in your ungodly, unproductive state, you will see the strongholds tumble from before your eyes. Instead of my always saying, *I must do this*, or *I don't see how I would make it out there on my own*, or *I don't want to be a statistic*, I started ripping myself away from weaknesses. I would say in tears: *I must change my situation; I can do this; a job will come from somewhere.* My faith in God reached out with such a violent force that it brought some real abundance into my life. Strongholds melted, mountains moved, and the enemy retreated to try to reload and return for a stronger attack. Oh, but by then I had tasted the beginning of the sweetness of success in God, and I wanted more. My drive to survive kicked in at such a level that if anything got in my way I took what I had learned in the night hours with God, about rooting out, pulling down, and destroying, and I gave it some blows. I wanted what I read about in the Scriptures. Just the appetizers were tasting good. I had not even gotten to the main course.

I began to thank those who opposed me and gave me pure hell. If they had not tried to take me out I would not have found the place I was in. Nothing, nothing mattered as much to me as when I would be with my Lord in the inner court and He would suspend me in His love, allowing me to feel something I had never even imagined in my life before. All I could think of was *give me more, give me more!* In fact, at that time in my life the person that had given me so much grief called me one night and here is what I told him. I said, "If I could, I would pay ten Egyptian women to come and be with you and give you your every thrill, because I just don't have time for you anymore." I was free through God opening my eyes to who He made me to be. I felt like I had scored the game's winning point from down court in the most important game of all time. Neither man nor woman could tell me anything. My God had let me taste just a bit of kingdom dinner. I was discovering who I was, whom I served, and what it all meant.

The eyes of my understanding were enlightened. All I want to do now is help someone else walk into the place where God has created all things well. I want to help because I am familiar with the torment, the turmoil, and the final state of devastation. God showed me how to pull myself up from the ashes of my circumstances. He showed me how to demolish the strongholds in my life and walk in the fullness of God. I just want to share so others too can enjoy life in the quality sent to us. Now, if you demolish your own strongholds and pull down all those things that are enmity to godly survival, then why would you live with anyone else's strongholds? Why make yourself victim to someone else's strongholds if you have worked on your own? Freeing yourself from your strongholds will help you to recognize another's strongholds, but it will also enable you to not become captive of their fortresses.

People have different unacceptable reasons for why they do what they do to us, but we do not have to aide them in it. Here are a few for starters: childhood experiences, educational failures, racism, greed, lust, inferiority, family cycles, curses, and so many other things are reasons why people do what they do. I now say let *them* live with their misery, not me. Let them realize that the causes of their inferiority do not give them permission to engage in inflicting pain, abuse, or destruction onto another. We are to help the lost, not join them.

I want to look at how God, in His Word, felt about the strongholds people were experiencing and what was done. Let's go to Zephaniah 3:6: "I have cut off nations; their strongholds are demolished. I have left their streets deserted, with no one passing through. Their cities are destroyed; no one will be left—no one at all" (NIV). Jerusalem had done wicked things during these times. They were not serving God based on His plan for their lives. Are you? Jerusalem was living beneath the high plan of God because of the idol worship and just the general forsaking of the way. Verse 2 of the same chapter says that "she [Jerusalem] does not trust in LORD." Wow, God is stating that this is not acceptable. We must trust God to be all that He says He is. We must allow Him to take care of us. Now God shows directly where He will go because of the disobedience; in verse 6 their strongholds are demolished. God will demolish the strongholds, which are at the heart of the matter. You have to root out and pull down strongholds in order to be the men and women God intended you to be. Start now. Make a commitment to pull down your own strongholds. You know what they are, I don't. God knows what they are, and He is here to help you.

Because of how long we have been constructing these strongholds, many times they are bigger than we are. This is why we need supernatural help to pull them down. But it feels so wonderful. The psalmist David said that the Lord's "lovingkindness is better than life" (Ps. 63:3). Yes, He is so lovingly kind in how He helps us overcome these strongholds that it is so much better than what life is without Him in it.

When we pull down on strongholds we actually exert force onto something else to draw it towards the force. In other words, you can pull down something hanging on display because you no longer want it on display. Remember, God's people during Jeremiah's time had been guilty of forsaking the true God and worshiping idols and other ungodly forms. These things had to go. They could be displayed no more. It was time to pull them down. What have we displayed today in our lives? Many times we display that our God is a weak God. That God brought all this meanness and trouble to us. We show, by our agreement with bondage and forms of captivity, that God maybe isn't a strong tower.

We portray to the world what is in fact not God at all. We allow situations of man, what man does to us, betrayal, neglect, homelessness, unemployment, being fatherless or motherless, molestation, and other shameful conditions to dictate who God is for all the world to see. We show Him as weak and not fulfilling His Word when we don't abide in the strength, the abundance, the freedom, the joy, and the peace He says is ours. We do this when our worship is focused on our situation and not on who our source is. People say, *Look at poor Sally, she is in a very bad way.* It is time to pull those things down if that is what you display. Pull down telling the world how the devil has the power to take you out or to snuff the life right out of you. Pull down the attitudes that allow the devil to say he won. We can pull down all those things and show who we really serve. I came to this juncture in life. It was not easy. But despite everything that had happened to me; despite every dream I ever dreamed being destroyed; despite the fact that I felt I was so far down I would never see light again, I decided that either God is true or He is not. Either God would display who He is in my life or it wasn't worth all of this. So I pulled it down. I pulled down the junk that was on display. I began to display only Him.

Pulling down all the things that had for so long displayed my heart's position was very, very difficult. You see, I had shown how the devil was beating me up for so long that the enemy was used to being on display in my life. Oh, but when I pulled one devil down from display in my life then Christ could be seen. Pulling him down made people wonder. I heard whispers like: "How in the world can she be that happy?" or "It is just a matter of time. She will break and end up in an institution because her level of joy—it is not normal." When I pulled all those things down that did not belong on display in my life in the first place, things changed for me. Pull down the mess that controls you. I began to test the Word that says, "Draw nigh to God, and he will draw nigh to you" (James 4:8, KJV). Pulling down a display that held its stance for thirty years took effort and a will to live above the horror. If you cannot pull down the things that are holding you back, you can never go forward.

You must seize it, take it by the throat and not allow ungodly strongholds to handicap your life any longer. God will take care of you if He is allowed. He can't if you can't let Him. If you knew right now how good it truly is to allow God to take care of you and to prove who He truly is in your life, you would tear through brick walls and high towers, take your strongholds, and destroy them all. Without faith it is impossible to please God, so stretch out on your faith in God and walk with Him. Listen to God and obey only what He says to *you*; not what He has said to me or other people. No two situations of bondage are alike, so you need to know Him for yourself. The only thing that is the same for all of us is that He gets good pleasure from giving all of us the kingdom. He so loved us all. (See John 3:16.) He is ready to do for us what He has done for others. He is waiting on us. I wish it had not taken three decades of my life to accept this, but oh it feels good now. I am living as if those three decades never happened. I mean it. Sometimes now I actually forget that I had such a dreadful past. I guess the root of my experience is gone and strongholds have been demolished.

Have you ever felt the pressure a dentist must exert in order to pull out a bad tooth? It seems at first that there is such a tremendous pressing in. It is like he presses so hard into it that he pulls it out. That is what I want to pause on now. You need to press so hard as if your life depended upon it because it does, and then pull those things right out of your life. Don't work on pulling out the mote in your brother's eye but work on the beam in your own eye. (See Matthew 7:3–5.) You will see better when you do. You will see that God did not call you to be weak, frail, unproductive, and accepting of abuse and evil deeds from others in your life. Let's summarize at this point: root out or pluck out the ungodly weaknesses in your life that cause unproductive living. Next, when the roots are visible to you and you have them in your grip, pull down their strongholds on your life and live in the abundance God has ordained for you.

Chapter 6

Step 3: Destroy

S TEP 3 IS to destroy. We are destroying weapons when we allow ourselves to be used effectively. Anything in our lives that restricts or does not permit the peaceful, loving abiding of our Savior robs us. The attitude, behavior, or handicaps that make us accept these things must be destroyed if we are ever to be totally restored.

I had heard for years that all I needed to do was destroy or kill off the emotional handicaps in my life. How do we do that? How do we really destroy the emotional upheavals we have developed an addictive behavior to? We form bonds with our weaknesses and fears. To fully understand how to destroy those types of unproductive bonds, here is what I have. In the natural sense, things get destroyed when they are taken over by something greater, stronger, or wiser than them. So then, people destroy an insect very easily because their foot is naturally bigger and simply smashing or squashing an insect kills or destroys it. Sometimes what is bigger or stronger does not do the destroying. Sometimes what is stronger yet, not bigger or greater, can destroy.

There is one more category I would like to mention. That

which is greater, stronger, wiser, or more clever can do the destroying. Therefore, we need something bigger, stronger, and wiser than our handicaps and inhibitions to destroy them. David as a little shepherd boy was not bigger or stronger than Goliath. But he was wiser, or smarter, in that David knew that the God of Israel was faithful to get him out of past dangers and would prevail in this case also. (See 1 Samuel 17.) So let's summarize it: in order to destroy those unneeded strongholds in our lives we need the bigger, the greater, the stronger, and the wiser than all the strongholds. Only God's Word provides that. Remember, God is so powerful that Jesus lead captivity captive. (See Ephesians 4:8.) He can enable us to be free of our captivities. We have all that is stronger, greater, and wiser at our disposal anytime. We just need to use it. Apply the Word of God to your situation in order to destroy the plans and vices of the devil.

All through the Old Testament we find the children of Israel instructed to destroy molten images, false idols, altars of Baal, idols of gold, and the like. These things should not be in our lives either, but many times they are. We set up people and things as our god. We trust them more than we do God. We fear what they can do to us, or better said, what they may take away from us. God is our source. When we find the courage to take God at His Word and allow Him to take care of us, the faith we place in Him pleases Him. For many years I thought of all the things I would have to do without on one income. I also thought life was so swell that being on my own would lessen my quality of living. I trusted more that the evil I was in and the bad circumstances could be better for me than total dependence on my Savior. I stayed for the wrong reasons. Some situations can be restored, blessed by God, and survive. Many times God does the miraculous and mends relationships. He is the God of revival. Dead bones can live again. We just need to live close enough to God to know which situation specifically we have.

My reasons for acceptance in these matters actually reflected the wrong things. First, I said that God brought this into my life to teach me; these trials were from Him. Nothing could have been further from the truth. Secondly, my behavior showed that I trusted in my own way more than I trusted that God was my source. The quality of my life certainly changed when I changed the situation. My life gained real quality when I did something about my own crippling emotions and allowed God to work in my life. When I began to destroy my own destructive behavior, true quality of life came and introduced itself to me. I found out that what I thought was quality before was painted lies and pretense. The things in my life, heart, and behavior would have destroyed me had I not come to my senses and destroyed them first. Thank God I did. Don't spare any of the devices that crippled you. All of them must go. Many successful people weaken in relationships in such a way that is unbelievable. There are people who have achieved greatness, careers, houses, lands, and much material wealth in life but are weakened when things go wrong. They accept abuse and mis-use while pretending things are OK. Determined people will fight to destroy the things in their life that hold them back. I fought for many years because I too was a determined person. But I did not know how to destroy the crippling behavior until it was revealed to me.

Let's talk about how to destroy these things. What does it really take to reclaim the victorious living according to the Scriptures? Let's look at one of the stories regarding Saul to understand fully destroying the characteristics that handi-cap us and make us failures. In 1 Samuel 15, Saul was told to utterly strike and destroy the Amalekites and all their possessions (v. 3). Why? Because of all the great harm they had done to God's people (v. 2). They laid awake for them at times and ambushed God's people when they were weary. Saul launched his attack on the Amalekites but decided to spare what looked good to him. He spared King Agag and the best of the sheep and other animals. He destroyed only what looked ill or evil with his natural eyes (v. 9). You see what Saul did spare was heard later with the bleating of the sheep in the background as a charge against him (v. 14). The things we spare because of how it looks to us will always be a bleating in the background. We will always have the reminder that we have part of the situation continually with us. The bleating of the abuse haunts us until we fight the good fight of faith until these things are totally destroyed.

Why continue to do the things that make us weak and not strong? We destroy weaknesses when we turn to the strength extended to us. Our inner souls cry out for better and we have to suppress the cry in order to continue. We lie to ourselves. If we are called to be conquerors, why are we conquered? Many times the devil flaunts who he is while the people of God cry and plead for the abuse to stop. We are the ones able to stop the abuse. We can destroy the yoke of bondage that we built around us through faith in God. If I had known that the quality of life I experienced when I decided to change my circumstances would happen, I would not have thirty years to tell you about. Although I was alone for years after I initiated the change, it did not bother me. As I learned how to root out, pull down, and destroy the things that made me so handicapped I became happier and happier. Some people went out just to say they had a date. I was so happy that those things did not matter to me. I was so emerged in what my inner woman was learning I kept saying, *Give me more of this.* Life got brighter than the morning sun to me.

When the horrible thoughts and the pains of the past kept trying to barge in on my new life I applied what God revealed to me. I took each thought and rooted it out of my mind by forcing my thoughts to be about good things. I pulled down, or broke down, anything that was not of God. If it did not promote healthy, productive living, it had to go. It had to be pulled down, and I placed my ways and godly behavior on the plans for my bright future. I destroyed those things by living contrary to their effect that could have existed. I talked every day as though I never had a problem. I destroyed the plagues of the past by opening myself up to love and loving. I prayed for those that had harmed me. I prayed because it was a very hard thing to do. That is how I knew I needed to do it. I prayed every night until it was easy and until I really was praying for them and not just saying words. I wanted so badly for Mark 11:25 to be a reality in my life that no matter who had harmed me I was going to forgive.

> Therefore I say to you, whatever things you ask when you pray, believe that you receive them, and you will have them. And whenever you stand praying, if you have anything against anyone, forgive him, that your Father in heaven may also forgive you your trespasses.
> —MARK 11:24–25

The way to get your petitions and prayers answered is to first remember to let go of anything you have against anyone. There are many things that we cannot take with us on the journey to total restoration. Among all of them, unforgiveness will derail you each time. I did not destroy the ugly head of unforgiveness in me because I am a nice person. I did not just decide to wake up, be kind, and forgive the abuse, shame, and horrible years. I made a mental list of things I wanted from God. I then assessed the things that would get me there and the things that would hinder me. Well, living so that I would get everything I want in life according to the Scriptures was far more important to me than living in the past. You see, it depends on how bad you want something and the cost you will pay to get there.

At first, the very thought of forgiving the wrong done to me made me choke up. It just did not seem possible to look away from so much wrong done to me. However, when I thought about what I would get if I did forgive and what I would never have if I didn't, it made all the difference. Many people say that they don't like to be bossed around by other mean, dominating people. Yet we don't realize that when we don't forgive someone that person is bossing our lives. Their power over our lives denies us the ability to go where we want in life because we have to stay right where we are and hold them while all the time holding ourselves. While holding them there we can't go anywhere either. So, they are bossing you. You have no control over where you go in life until you let go of all those who have harmed you in life. The enemy uses unforgiveness as an instrument to outwit us. It is one of his devices. But we are not ignorant of Satan's devices. (See 2 Corinthians 2:11.)

When I realized I wanted to decide where I go, it was a simple decision. I prayed: *Lord show me how to let this person go.* I needed someone to show me how to not let thirty years of horrible mistreatment matter. That is when the words "forgetting those things which are behind" were explained to me (Phil. 3:13). *Forgetting means to neglect*, I heard the Spirit say. Neglect those things that are in the past. Don't water them. Don't nourish them. They will die without water. The water is my attention, my thoughts, and my time. Don't give any part of you to the past and it will wither from lack. *Destroy* means to demolish. Another way to demolish an unforgiving spirit is to assess its long-term effect on you as an individual. When you become aware of its deadly poison spreading and keeping you from life's fullness, it should be enough for you to let go.

Destruction does not just happen. You don't wake up one morning and all the negativity and the components of the emotional handicap just disappear. Even in war, force is exerted to take out the enemy. I believe this is why we are told that the violent taketh by force. That powerful force is our faith. Faith is a violent force in that it tears through everything in its path to bring about the hope that is sought after. Faith lets nothing stand in its way. Remember, faith can't even see things in the physical realm because it is a spiritual force having only spiritual vision. We must have faith in God as we take every step on the journey of restoration. I wish I could tell you that it happens overnight. I truly wish I could, but it does not. Not the type of restoration I am sharing about. You can experience salvation and be restored to fellowship with God. There is, however, a deeper restoration needed for those of us with deeply embedded abuses and scars that were inflicted upon us by relationships during childhood, adolescent years, and/or as adults. There is a work to be done in order to destroy the effects Satan has tried to mark us with.

One of the things that needed destroying in my life, after this long, difficult relationship, was that I needed to cease blaming myself. I have never believed in failure, or not making it, at anything. So, for years I thought that there were things I needed to do to save this marriage. Since I refuse to fail at anything, I felt having a failed marriage could not happen. I felt as if I was failing. The truth is; someone was failing me.

There is a big difference. Guilt is usually one of our very first visitors, among many, that search us out and say things like, *Here is what you should have or could have done and things would have been different.* Doing certain things differently sometimes does help. However, your doing things differently does not change the other person. It merely changes you to the point that you allow yourself more adjustments for what is being done. As a victim, feeling guilt is par for the course. In other words, certain abuses produce a set series of afflictions, and guilt is one of them. Of course we all need someone to blame for the horrible experiences of life and our inner search for perfection and acceptance prompts us to say, *I know who is to blame; I am.* Thus, say hello to one of longest guilt-trips known to mankind.

On the road of guilt you find a lot of help to stay there. You are verbally accused for the actions of someone else. People sometimes say that you drove them to abuse you. Well, get real, if others are blaming you, do you need to jump on the wagon and blame you too? People act according to the structure of character they have to draw from.

> But each one is tempted when he is drawn away by his own desires and enticed.
>
> —JAMES 1:14

It took me a long, long time to find that out, so I will say it again in a slightly different way: when a person is in any given situation they act and draw from the storehouse of goods that is within them. This was an alarming fact for me. If the goods in inventory are from the enemy, people will consult the enemy on which goods to use in certain situations. Similarly, in my situation the goods in my storehouse were from God, so I consulted God. Thus, godly behavior to survive surfaced.

Don't allow people to blame you for their actions. They may not have known the proper response to your actions, but their actions are a direct result of who they are. Destructive things and desires that were not destroyed in their own lives were consulted. That is why it is so important that we destroy all the ungodly strongholds in our lives. If we don't destroy them we will eventually consult them later in other situations and relationships. This is why you see people making the same error over and over in life. They are consulting the same crippling characteristics from the past. Let me tell you I know this for a fact. God cast out many nations from before His people to ensure their safe passageway. (See Deuteronomy 7:1–2.) Our safe passageway lies in us making sure we destroy the obstructing behavior that binds us to a life that does not declare who our Savior really is. I heard of a woman once who kept having mental breakdowns. She had several. But each time she was released from a treatment facility she would go right back to the person that helped to put her there in the first place. If a person could not be kind and loyal to you when you are at your best, what makes you think that in a weak, emotionally frail state you would gain their affection? We are just not thinking. In the latter state, weak and dependent, you are less desirable and more fitted for misuse than before. You don't know how to accept who you are and love yourself, so why should anyone else?

Destroy the things that make you weak and emotionally crippled, no matter how deep you need to go. Address those issues of fear to be by yourself, not having a true father figure, or abandonment and other abuses. Whatever makes you go there deal with and destroy it. Smash it and take it out, but make sure you use God's method to do so and not your own. This does not always mean you must end the relationship.

Sometimes we just need to end how we respond to things. Replace the weak, frail things in your life with strength, endurance, and perseverance. Your methods fail. God's methods are eternal and sure. You must resolve yourself to the fact that you have to destroy certain things or those things will destroy you. A very wise person would have said this: "If you don't reprove the wrong, the wrong will eventually reprove you." Let me tell you, reproof is sometimes hard to swallow. However, it's better than hearing life scream back at you that all you went through really was not necessary if you had just conquered your ills rather than let them hang around.

Chapter 7

Step 4: Throw Down

L ET'S REVIEW THE three previous steps on our journey to total restoration. They are root out, pull down, and destroy. Now we move on to throw down. Another version of saying it is this: root out = plucking out, pull down = break down, destroy = demolish, and throw down = overturn.

You must now overturn everything in your life that has exalted itself above God. As we place emphasis on other things and people as our source, those mental and emotional gods and idols must be overturned. I will explain in greater detail what is meant by overthrow or overturning as it relates to being restored. When a house that is in bad condition is restored, the things that stood out as damaged are overturned by the repairs or restoration. The new components replace the old. Old kingdoms are overturned by the new kingdoms that replace them. The old, crippling effects that ruled the old kingdom are no longer ruling over the new kingdom. Thus, we are to overthrow the issues and components that crippled us in the first place, as they are revealed to us. We overthrow them by eliminating their power over us. We can do all things through Christ who grants us the strength (Phil 4:13). Those old powers made us weak and made us distrust and doubt our outcome. We must overthrow these issues in our lives or we lock ourselves into bondage to unwanted situations. Remember, Jesus was anointed to heal the brokenhearted, to liberate the captives, and to set at liberty the oppressed (Luke 4:18). Apply the Word of God to overthrow all strongholds in your life. Nothing and no person should be on display over God in your life. Do not allow worship of any false gods; overthrow them just as God instructed Israel (Exod. 23:24–25). There are a lot of spiritual Amorites, Hittites, Perizzites, Canaanites, Hivites, and Jebusites in our lives that need overthrowing. God told Israel to utterly destroy those foreign nations in verse 25. We are spiritual Israel and we should utterly destroy foreign rule over our lives with the power and Word of God.

Overthrow peoples' strongholds in your life. Do not let them, or anything, make you less the child of the King than He intended you to be. If you don't overthrow them, trust me, they will eventually overthrow you. I will give you a couple examples of people who allowed their circumstances to overthrow them by not acting to overthrow the devilish hold on their lives.

Remember the well-known story about the woman in Texas who ran down her husband with her car and killed him when she encountered him with his mistress? It was all over the news. One day, as I passed by my television, I noticed a clip was showing of the area outside a hotel. I remember watching this car as it kept running over a man until he was dead. I could not help but relate it to the night I was in a very similar Mercedes and had almost the exact same encounter. I remember gripping that steering wheel while voices shouted in my head, "Run them both down! Run them both down!" I can recall today as if it were yesterday how the voices got louder and louder trying to make me do something that would rob me of my own future. I was frightened and nervous and I felt forsaken and abandoned as I watched them. However, another voice was there that said, "Don't run them over. You have a future and a hope. Don't do it." As difficult as it was, I overturned or overthrew certain things out of my life that night. The lady from Texas was not so fortunate. She killed her husband that night and now has many years to spend in prison for doing it. So, if you don't overturn them, they will overturn you.

When I saw on television some of the awful, horrible things that woman endured it made me think of my past home and the things inflicted upon me. These were horrible things, leaving her emotionally raped and mentally scarred by someone she felt love for. However, had she overthrown what was being done to her in the earlier years of her life the night that stole her future could not have happened. My heart still weeps for her. But sometimes I wonder if I weep for her because she is a carbon copy of what could have happened to me. Could it be that I weep for her because I wish the freedom I found in Christ for us all? Or do I weep for her because I carry a burden for anyone facing those and other types of ills in life? Praise God for the grace to overturn those things in my life. For me, after that night in 1997, and some other awful things that followed, I ran with all the might my heart could muster up. I knew after that night I had to find a way to get out of this hellhole.

When 1997 had come and gone and years later I watched the news excerpts about that crime and the encounter, the tears fell from my face. I had made the right choice and ran straight into my Savior's arms for His help in overturning such things and protecting my future. I remain ever grateful and commissioned to go where I am supposed to go and help who

I am supposed to help. I was not spared that night, or of other dreadful events, just to put these things on a shelf and leave them there. It is like the night a man with a gun came up to me. We stood face to face and I knew he had every intention of killing me. The plan God had for my life, and the destiny I was sure to walk in, shouted so loud that night that that gunman could *not* shoot me. Instead, he shot the person with me. Somehow, I was spared from his rage. Soon after that night and the attempt on my life, I was called to a place that allowed me to hear the voice of the Lord and His call on my life to help and assist others. There was a call of destiny so loud that it overthrew everything else that should not be in my life.

I knew there was a God and I was going to find the peace He talks about in His Word. I had to experience it. I had to overthrow the things that were trying to rob me of the future God had for me. Life was trying to rob me of my opportunity to tell you this story from the comfort of my home. Satan would rather I told it from a prison cell, or not at all. After that horrible night, I wanted to be freer than ever before. I started fiercely searching for anything and everything that needed to be overthrown in my life. Those things did not come looking for me. I went looking for them. I could taste restoration. I knew that there was a good future for me, and that my ways were keeping me from enjoying it. I wanted to no longer be weak. Being saved and not being restored was still like death to me. To know something, see it, and not taste it for yourself is a very cruel position to be in. My desire and constant prayer to God for deliverance from the wretched, weak condition I was in caused an overthrowing era to begin in my life. No chains or lockdown could suppress it.

I received a call one day about a job in another state that I eventually took. At first, I did not see that this was just a step to lead me toward freedom. When one door closes you should always look for the one that opened. When one brook dries up, look for the next brook that is flowing with love. Like the prophet Elijah when the ravens no longer fed him and the brook dried up, God spoke and said, "[See], I have commanded [someone else] to sustain thee" (1 Kings 17:9, KJV). (See 1 Kings 17:1–9.) Let go of the dried-up brooks, and He will take care of you. Overturn the things that cause you to hold on to dried-up brooks or you will never see the miracles or experience the abundance that awaits you. Back in ancient times, and even today, people knew that in order to take over a kingdom, throne, or place of majesty you must overthrow the reigning kingdom. Two rulers cannot reign in the same place. You and I must overthrow the weaknesses that reign in the place where God wants strength and trust and faith to reign. If I were you, I would not wait another second. I would immediately begin to overthrow these ills. Set up the new in newness of life. This again was a command to the prophet Jeremiah to root out, pull down, destroy, and overthrow. This had to be done before building and planting could be successful. This tells us that the ground needed to be prepared for building and planting. Let's look at how we root out, pull down, destroy, and overthrow. Second Corinthians 10:4–5 states:

> For the weapons of our warfare are not carnal but mighty in God for pulling down strongholds, casting down arguments and every high thing that exalts itself against the knowledge of God, bring every thought into captivity to the obedience of Christ.

Let us park here in "overthrow" just a bit longer. There is more to be said since this is the final part of the dismantling process before we move on to build and plant. Anything not truly overturned will surface again in our lives. Every land that Israel was to possess had to be fully overthrown or they were not truly victorious. You are only victorious if the things keeping you from God's best are crushed out. When certain weak behaviors try to overthrow us we can render them powerless through faith in God. If you don't overthrow the most minute or smallest particle of unforgiveness from your heart it will overthrow you from kingdom benefits. Kingdom benefits became so important to me that I begged God to allow me to experience true forgiveness. It was a reality to me that I was not going to get anywhere unless I overthrew unforgiveness from my life. It had to go. It could not stay if I was to enter into the place I could envision. You too, must let go and forgive. Forgive them, she, he, it, they, and all. Overthrow the thoughts, the resentment, the vengeance, the evil wishes, and more because full and total restoration is worth it. It is a much sweeter, much more rewarding land to live in.

I have heard it said before that when Rome wanted to take over every providence they knew that they had to overthrow all the other kingdoms around them that reigned. Unless you overthrow the things that make you weak, frail, and unfit in life, you really don't reign at all. As my spiritual father has always said, "You are not a conqueror—you are more than conquered." So don't place those inherited weaknesses down gently— throw them down! Throw them down out of your life. Let the abundance you are meant to have rule and guide you into fullness of life. "Eye hath not seen, nor ear heard, neither have entered into the heart of man, the things which God hath prepared for them that love him"; enough to place their hand in His and say, *Lead me to the restoration that only you give* (1 Cor. 2:9, KJV). When the prophet Isaiah spoke on these terms he proclaimed that since the beginning of the world men have not heard or seen any God who acts for those who wait for Him (Isa. 64:4). God meets the person who has faith in Him and does righteousness. It is worth the overthrowing to really get to meet Him and embrace the divine reform you are destined for. You only have to believe and have faith that without it, it is impossible to please Him.

Chapter 8

Step 5: Build

I T IS MUCH easier to describe this step with pen on pad than
to complete the actual task. Step five is to build, construct,
or form. We must first complete the prior steps in our lives
before we can begin to build. If you start to build before rooting out, pulling down, destroying, and throwing down you will
be building on corrupt soil. You do not want to build on defective soil. Your ground must be free of these toxins or you will
always experience them corrupting your life and well-being
again and again. With Saul, the bleating of the sheep in the
background really told where he was with God. (See 1 Samuel
15:14.) The bleating will always be there unless you build on
pure clean soil.

Remember the dentist. He cleans everything out of the canal
before he refills it and seals it. The reason for this is that any
bacteria left in the canal will create a worse condition to deal
with. This is what happens to us at times. We leave the debris
for so long that it becomes even more painful and difficult to
deal with. If we deal with things when we should, they don't
become giants to deal with. However, if you have waited until
things are like giants in your life, like I did, remember that no

Goliath can stand and defy the holy man or woman of God when they know who their source is.

Never build your house on the sand. Always build on a solid foundation so that it can withstand the storms and the winds that beat against you. Jesus is the Master Builder. Build things anew in your life. Replace the locust-eaten territories of your life with newness. Structure your living with the things that produce abundance of joy and peace. Do not try to build this yourself. You can't. In order to build the life that I write about here it takes supernatural help and natural submission of one's will. Think of a young child with lots of little building blocks as he is working hard trying to build something. Now think of your own life and what it is you have wanted to build and have all these years. What are the things that help you accomplish the building you desire? What are the things that will derail you from ever getting there? Make certain you build on the right foundation.

I decided a long time ago that I would never allow another person's actions to dictate my behavior. My dreams and desires meant enough to me to go after them, and that is what I found grace and strength to do. I did not know that in my life I would encounter all the Amalekites, Goliaths, and other challenges that came my way. What I did know is that the land had to be cleared if I would ever know true restoration. Certain things had to go. I first had to come to God and believe that He is God and He rewards those who seek Him with their whole heart. I understood why Miriam danced once she and the Israelites crossed the Red Sea. (See Exodus 15:20–21.) I was determined to dance my triumph out too. I wanted to dance in the victory of knowing my Redeemer lives. As you continue to build, onlookers may not fully understand what is being structured before them. However, you and your Savior know that a temple for God to dwell in is being restored.

Since the beginning of days God just wanted a place where He and His creation could fellowship. When the children of Israel were traveling toward the Promised Land they had a tent in which God's presence dwelt. The tabernacle provided a place for the Israelites to meet with God. Then Solomon in all his wisdom built an absolutely elegant, amazing temple where God was to dwell and the high priests would come and offer for the people. In Old Testament times there had always been a literal place for the presence of God. But we are spiritual Israel and we are the temple of God (2 Cor. 6:16). Natural Israel had physical buildings where the presence of God could be found, but this was not God's ultimate plan for mankind. The Old Testament provided a shadow of good things to come (Heb. 10:1). None of these buildings for housing God's presence fulfilled the divine plan and purpose of God. These were brick and mortar or tent buildings that only allow us to see God's planned purpose that lead to the real temples where God wanted to dwell in His people. He wants us totally restored as living stones, being built up a spiritual house, a holy priesthood, to offer up spiritual sacrifices acceptable to God through Jesus Christ (1 Pet. 2:5). We must be built up according to the right plan with Jesus Christ Himself as the Chief Cornerstone (1 Pet. 2:6–7).

Biblical history describes the period after Babylonian captivity, the period that is considered the return of the Jewish exiles, as a turbulent period. Though some were returning from exile this period is considered turbulent because captivity or bondage scars its victims to some degree. Many times we only view the actual bondage as turbulent misery when in fact, the period after the storm is often more difficult. Think about the cleanup after a hurricane. It is horrific to even begin to address the devastation and rebuild what has been destroyed. But rebuild we must. No matter what our scaring is from, we must rebuild. It is essential and a priority to rebuild.

Failing to rebuild sends the wrong message and basically is just the wrong thing to do. When we don't rebuild, our statement is that the thing beat us, it conquered us, and we did not conquer it. We are saying to the world that its evil and corruption won. The worst of lands, if nourished, tilled, and properly treated can produce again. Someone has to see the worth in the land. This is what God sees in us and this is why God's message is to build. Build a place that He can dwell in. Not a tent or structure like in Old Testament times, but a temple not made with hands.

Sometimes the period following a severe storm is the most difficult, like in the period following the captivity. Many things had to be reestablished—even customs and traditions. The temple had been destroyed and laid in ruins. Therefore, certain customs of worship and traditions could not be carried out. God spoke through the prophet Haggai, letting the people know that they had to rebuild a place of worship. Also there were blessings that were withheld from them because they had neglected God's house. So much had to be reestablished that the people actually found it easier to rebuild their own houses and let the house of God go unbuilt. Haggai 1:3–11 tells the account of how the prophet Haggai admonished the people about their neglect of God's house. It was very difficult at first for the people because rebuilding sometimes requires more effort than you realize. The work had been abandoned after the first attempt to rebuild the temple for more than sixteen years (Ezra 4:23). Due to opposition from the outside and discouragement from within the King of Persia issued a command to stop rebuilding the temple. The work to rebuild God's house did not resume again until the time of King Darius of Persia with Haggai's message to the people. Again, keep in mind that not having a place of worship meant that customs and practices usually carried out in the temple were let go. Opposition was strong and caused the restoration to cease (Ezra 4).

Many times in our spiritual lives similar opposition is present, thus making the task of rebuilding more difficult. In fact, just as the rebuilding had ceased because of the opposition in natural Israel we too many times find the task of rebuilding so hard that we quit applying the principles of God that lead to a restored life. I must encourage you, never stop seeking the restoration God wants for you. You must have confidence in God that He knows what He is doing even in the hardest times (Heb 10:35). Do not cast away your confidence for there is a great reward.

We must follow God's plan for our life because His plan leads us away from unproductiveness and into abundance. It is true in my own life that there were many times I felt God did not know what He was doing because my pain seemed more than I could take. Not having a local church or pastor made it seem even harder to understand my situation and the pain it brought with it. These times allowed me to develop a strong intimacy with God during many early morning hours (2 a.m. to 5 a.m.). I pursued who God claimed to be in His Word during those hours for years, and my faith paid off big time. I could now see with my spiritual vision the woman that God was developing. There were so many nights that my pain caused me to just break in tears profoundly. As I clung to God for dear life (trust me it was life or death) I began to learn that a lot of my pain came from my views on my situation. Now I don't mean that the things that happened to me were insignificant by any means. I am trying to tell you that how I looked at my past, present, and future caused the more intense pain. Let me say this, if you put on blue sunglasses everything will look blue. Things are not really blue but the glasses you are looking with cause what you see. Well, if you put on the devil's glasses of torment about your life everything will look tormenting. But if you put on God's views about your life you will see yourself as God sees you. I was tormenting myself with the way I viewed my life more than anything. You must look with the eyes of the heart being enlightened, that you may know what is the hope to which He has called you (Eph. 1:18).

Hebrews 12:2 tells us to look to Jesus, the Author and Finisher of our faith. I finally stopped keeping my eyes on the problem and focused on the solutions found in the Word of God. You must let the past go and break free. This is the only way to experience restoration totally. In the Book of Haggai God encouraged the prophet to let the people know that their hard and difficult times are because they have not rebuilt God's temple (Haggai 1:3–9). As the people of God many times we try to work on other things and not our own buildings. We are the temple of the Holy Spirit, and if this temple is not restored according to Scripture, we too continue to have hard times because restoration or rebuilding has not taken place. In Haggai we see that God understood that people would be discouraged because the rebuilt temple may not be as big or glamorous as the first temple. Abuse, betrayal, and the storms of life make us believe similarly. We say or think that what we once had we will never have again. Perhaps what you wanted from life seemed to escape your best efforts. You and I think we had more in the past than what we look to in the future. How sad this thought is for those of us who feel this way. Never make such a negative comparison on your life because what is important is that the presence and glory of the Almighty abides with us. The Lord promises to fill it with His presence; He declared the glory of the latter house shall be greater than that of the former. His people needed to know this. The glory that is to come will outshine everything you thought you had. Restoration totally brings that level of glory. Solomon's temple was glorious, but God had a future temple in mind—one not made of stones and mortar. It is that of the restored life, a life so built on the things of God that the past, present, or anything in the future cannot overthrow it.

I had to rebuild my life with such determination that I often referred to the words of Paul just to find solace. I repeated many nights:

> Who shall separate [me] from the love of Christ? shall tribulation [abuse], or distress [pressures of my circumstances], or persecution [things that come against me], or famine [what I must do without]... [yet] in all these things [I conquered].
>
> —ROMANS 8:35–37, KJV

I conquered because it meant more to me to go over and possess the restored land than to stay in a corrupt, abused, and misused land. It became my goal in life to build all things new. Then I read that He makes all things new (Rev. 21:5). He tells us not to remember the former (Isa. 43:18). You will never get fully restored living in the corruption of the past. Move on to a land that is plenteous. Build again. That is what you do when you get loose. Go somewhere, get with God, and began to build again. Build so much that those who look on will say, "How did he get all that from what life handed him?" Yes, build again and allow God to do what He does best, and that is to take care of you.

The only reason we feel that God is not taking care of us is because we won't allow Him to do it. I remember once I was crying. I cried, it seemed, until there were no more tears. I swelled my eyes, my face, and my lips. I just had one of the grandest, old, cry-your-eyes-out party with no one there but me. I felt a need to explain to God why I was crying because I did not want God to think that I did not trust or believe in Him. I said, "God, I am not crying because I don't trust You. I do trust You, and it is not because I don't believe in You. I do." I needed Him to know that I was only crying because I was heavy from my situation. The load of my situation and circumstances had pressed me down so that I could not carry the load. Well, when I finished crying and explaining and explaining and crying, the Holy Spirit spoke gently to me, "If you are crying because something is heavy then you are carrying it and not God. You have your problems, and you have not given the problems to the Savior." That was an amazing thing for me. I had the problems, and I had not yet given them to Him. Had I given them away I could not possibly feel the weight. From that day on I understood better how we cast our burdens on the Lord because He cares for us (1 Pet. 5:7). I have not since that time reached back for my cares; I don't feel the weight from them anymore. I started allowing God to take care of me the way He wanted to. He desired to take care of me, and I had not been letting His care come through. I began to build again on the things that God wanted in my life. Building is a very important step in the formula of restoration. You can clear the land, uncorrupt the land, but if you never move on to put someone beautiful on it, there it stands barren or unproductive. You must build again. You can build again. You have the Master Builder in your life.

Again, I want to repeat, in the Book of Haggai, God encourages the prophet Haggai to let the people know that their hard and difficult times are because they have not rebuilt God's temple. (See Haggai 1:1–11.) We are the temple of the Holy Spirit and if this temple is not restored according to Scripture we too will continue to have hard times. Further in the story, God realizes that the people will be discouraged because the restored temple may not be as big, glamorous, or have as much splendor and glory as the first temple (Hag. 2:3). Abuse, betrayal and many storms in life make us believe similarly. We say or think that what we once had we will never have again. Never make such a negative comparison. What's important is that the presence and glory of the Almighty abides within us. The Lord promises to fill us with His presence. Again, He declared "the glory of this latter temple shall be greater than the former" (Hag. 2:9). His people needed to know this. The glory that is to come will out-shine everything you thought you had. Restoration totally brings that level of glory. Solomon's temple was very glorious, but God had a future temple in mind; one not made of stones and mortar, but of the restored life. A life so built on the things of God that the neither the past, present, nor or anything in the future could overthrow.

Restoration starts with a vision. You must envision in your heart that it is yours to be restored or whatever is needed to have God's original plan in your life. You must with faith purpose to have what God designed, just like when someone sees an old house and they stand and envision it restored. Know in your heart and declare it for yourself from the beginning. Men restore things to their former beauty and intended purpose. God knows the hurts, harm, and persecution that damaged His original blueprint, and He is the only one capable of guiding us back from emotionally scarred bondage to the abundance we were meant to live in. No matter how many years the locusts have eaten or stolen from you, if you allow Him to take care of you the latter shall exceed the former. It will exceed what you thought you had.

Let's talk about building some more. This is such a vital step. In fact, I have observed that many people, once free from bondage of their circumstances, don't really become very productive Christians again because they fail to build. I have seen some fall away due to their failure to build again. This is why we must not stop when rooting out, pulling down, destroying, and throwing down are done. There is still work to do. "Build" is to "prepared land" as "fly" is to "airplane." What good is an airplane if it can't fly? Likewise, what good are our vessels if they can't be built up for a habitation of the Spirit?

At first I too found it very hard to build again, and when I realized my own inability to rebuild myself I sought God for the strength and faith to go on. If you seek Him, you will find Him and He will bring you back again from your captivity (Deut. 4:29). Once you are out of that captivity you must build again. Otherwise, you give the circumstances you came out of too much credit. Don't allow those things to take you out. Remember the words from back in the early colonies when Patrick Henry said, "Give me liberty or give me death." I say, "Give me restoration or things will be like death." Give me restoration totally, nothing else will do. I love these words so much that I must end this chapter with, "The glory of this latter temple shall be greater than the former" (Hag. 2:9). This latter glory can only be revealed when we build a temple in which God can abide. He said that if we abide in Him and His Words abide in us we can ask what we will and it shall be granted (John 15:7). I have started to use my abiding rights. I asked Him to build me up to only know and enjoy the things of God. I sought with all my heart as the prophet Jeremiah spoke and I found Him (Jer. 29:13). I decided to trade in all the ashes of my circumstances (the painful memories) for the beauty of truly knowing Him. I craved a level of restoration that could not be quenched by any substitution. Nothing could satisfy my craving for real restoration except being totally restored. I could not be fooled by pretense, even if it were my own.

We know when the wounds of our scarred past have not healed. The pain of what was experienced still exists. Unless you truly build again there remains no chance for total restoration. A land properly cleared of debris is just vacant land without being put to productive use. Build something or display something, just do not resolve to do nothing. I have seen fields or vacant lots where the land is used to grow beautiful grass to be used as sod for someone else's benefit. That is why I continue to say, *yes, yes we are loosed,* but what you need to do after you get loose is get restored totally. You belong to the wise Master Builder. Even in the New Testament the words of the prophets were brought back to the hearts and minds of the people reminding them of God's intent for them. It reads: "After this I will return And will rebuild the tabernacle of David, which has fallen down; I will rebuild its ruins, And I will set it up" (Acts 15:16). Our ruins are to be rebuilt. We are that tabernacle now in the last days. Studying and applying His Word is the only way that we become truly rebuilt again. When you look at the ruined areas of your life don't despair. Full restoration is not a job just for you to do. God understands and knows that you are dependent upon Him. You provide the faith, will, and obedience. The Master Builder does the work.

Remember the things we destroyed in step three. Never rebuild the things you have already destroyed. Don't make the same mistakes again and again. Don't repeat the cycle that got you there in the first place. This is what Paul warned the Galatians not to do. Paul said that "if [you] build again those things which [you] destroyed, [you] make [yourself] a transgressor" (Gal. 2:18). After my extreme captivity it seems that my thoughts and desires were going to overthrow me and lead me headfirst into similar relationships. But the eyes of my understanding were enlightened because I stayed before Him. I sought more of Him and less of anyone else. I became so acquainted with Him that I began to be able to detect all the counterfeits that came my way.

Let me explain further. People who specialize in identifying counterfeit money don't study counterfeit money, they study real, or valid, money. They become so acquainted with the real money that they can immediately spot a counterfeit. Learn of Him so that you don't repeat the same mistakes. Hide His Word away in your heart so that you don't sin against Him or yourself. (See Psalm 119:11.) Learn of the right way in order to detect the wrong elements. We sometimes repeat our horrors and build on the wrong things because we did not truly come to a place where our recognition of the right things was exercised. I would have been taken by a landslide many times, but my constant persistence to learn of a better way made me slow down. The slowing process brought recognition of what I was being offered the next time. Do not build on the wrong foundation and become repeat violators of what you know to be counterfeit. Through the words of the prophet Amos it was declared that on that day (we are in that day) He will raise up and repair the ruins and rebuild the relationship as it should be. (See Amos 9:11.)

Chapter 9

Step 6: Plant

W HY IS THIS the last step provided to the prophet of the amazing restoration plan? Let's review again, since each step is equally important: root out, pull down, destroy, throw down, build, and now to plant. Every nation that stood in God's people's way He had an overthrowing plan for them. Those nations and what was in His people's hearts had to go through the process proclaimed either in part or whole. It was even proclaimed by the prophet Jeremiah that the plan originally included this same formula against His people because of their disobedience. Jeremiah 31:28 is just one of the many passages that let us know this alarming truth:

> And it shall come to pass, that as I have watched over them to pluck up [root out], to break down, to throw down, to destroy, and to afflict, so I [God] will watch over them to build and to plant, says the Lord.

There will be no more sour grapes as in the past. There will always be tests and trials. However, as we are now planted in those things revealed by the Word, we can say that "He restores my soul" (Ps. 23:3). Surely, if we follow the divine plan for total restoration, "goodness and mercy shall follow [us] all the days of [our lives] (Ps. 23:6).

One definition of *plant* is "to set in the ground or set firmly in place." Webster's definition is "to establish." Just the mere thought of being so settled and established in all that God had revealed to me seemed mind boggling. Embracing what I had learned while trying to rebuild and move on seemed a painful task. I then realized that He was not telling me to plant anything at all because I cannot plant myself, but as I provide the soil or the heart of obedience, He would plant me. I took a deep breath when I realized He would do the planting. Not that I was off the hook; I still had a willing part to do in the whole process of restoration.

Plant means to establish and settle a thing or something into a place. The Word says:

> The God of all grace, who called us to His eternal glory by Christ Jesus, after you have suffered a while, perfect, establish, strengthen, and settle you.
>
> —1 PETER 5:10

Standing our test and trials is the suffering part, not suffering the things God did not send to us. So let's read it again this way, after you have stood your test and trials. He will perfect you, plant you, strengthen you, and plant you deeper. Open up your heart and let the planting began. The rooting out was the most painful because anytime you mess with the root of something it involves deep digging. So you endured the rooting out and all the other steps. Now, just let God plant the right seeds that need to be there for the kingdom and your sake.

God used illustrations about physical plants many times to help me understand what He was doing with me. There was a tree in my front yard once that was growing bent over to one side due to a strong windstorm that had come through the area. Even after the storm ended the tree continued to bend closer and closer to the ground. It looked ugly growing that way. It did not beautify the house or the yard. Well, a couple of years later I hired a young man to do some yard work who said, "I know just what that tree needs." It needed to be allowed to grow straight upright while being planted properly. This young man took a rope and drove a stake in the ground, wrapped the rope around the tree and back to the stake. The tree stood upright. Now it is growing straight and beautiful because it is planted properly. Because it was a young, tender tree when the storm hit, its planting structure was disrupted. It did not have the strong roots and trunk that the older trees had in the area so the storm affected it.

As we allow the new roots and good seeding of God's Word to go deeper we become strong trees planted by the rivers of water. The winds come and the rain beats upon our house but we stand because we are planted or built upon the rock (Matt. 7:25). Plant the right characteristics within your heart. Plant good thoughts. Find something good to think about no matter how many bad things you know. Philippians 4:8 tells us what things to think on or meditate on.

Plant forgiveness deep down so that it is in there to stay. Don't allow any bleating of the unforgiveness to ever reoccur or resurface. Plant peaceful living. Become more than a conqueror, instead of being conquered. Plant strength and courage and do "not grow weary while doing good, for in due season [you] shall reap" (Gal. 6:9).

Remember, "if you faint in the day of adversity, Your strength is small" (Prov. 24:10). I hated that with a passion. Just the very thought that I could have small strength made me angry. I don't like defeat in anything. Many times when I felt pressed the worst, I would remind myself that if you faint in the day of adversity you have small strength. Small strength just means it was too little or too small for what you needed victory over. I learned to look to those who have beautifully planted themselves in God and I learned from them. I followed the lives of those who were not overthrown by the force of the storm. I had to get planted where the devil could not have ownership of my life.

A plant has to abide in the soil that is producing the life-giving effects to the plant in order to survive. It must remain within this life-producing environment to live healthy. We are the branches, and we cannot bear fruit by ourselves.

> Abide in Me, and I in you. As the branch cannot bear fruit of itself, unless it abides in the vine, neither can you, unless you abide in Me.
>
> —JOHN 15:4

Stay (abide) attached to the vine. I knew that the wickedness of this world would take over my life if I did not go deep enough in God to dispel the horror life had sent my way. I heard the Holy Spirit say, "You cannot beat the devil on his own turf. Stay with me, you are on the winning side." My pain told me something different. My pain and tears were telling me to do something about all this awful mess. My pain said, *Get back, get back, get them back for old and new.* I learned that I could not become who God wanted me to be by consulting my past about my present obstacles. I could not reach a good future consulting with my past torments. The Spirit said, "Draw nigh to Me and I will draw nigh to you." (See James 4:8.) My pain cried louder, and it told me things that made sense, things like: *You are a fool to forgive someone for ruining thirty-plus years of your life. They are laughing at you, the world is laughing at you. Remember, people thought you would crack up and be institutionalized for the remainder of your life.* My pain kept talking to me every time I tried to plant the good.

Then one day it clicked. The mental list I had made many years ago, of all the abundance I wanted to experience, came back to me. I began to see a better life and the visions of double joy and peace that passes any understanding overwhelmed my thinking. I again assessed the requirements for getting me to where I wanted to be. I identified that the pain was my flesh trying to prevent me from entering into the life God wanted me to have. My flesh was yelling in pain to do something about what had been done to it. So I did. I took all my cares, every single one of the hurts, tears, fears, sleepless nights, thoughts of torment, joblessness, and all and gave them to my Savior. My flesh would try to consult the pain of my past and invite me to be a part of the party. Instead of giving in I began to let my pain know that it had to go and see Jesus about the things that were done to me. They belonged to Him now. I didn't have them anymore so it was no use visiting me with the pains of the past. I had things to do, places to go, people to see, and a faithful God to serve. I started feeling the miraculous, marvelous splendor of being made whole. I loved not having to take sleeping pill after sleeping pill because I could not get to sleep for all the painful, Technicolor movies that were sent direct from the enemy to me. I needed no more sleep aids.

I learned that unforgiveness is a tool or instrument of the emotion that the devil uses to outwit us. Yes, unforgiveness is a clever and evil tool that robs us. I can assure you from my close walk with God that much forgiving is far more powerful than vengeance and compassion is much greater than your own wrath. Only when you toss everything aside for the joy of knowing God and achieve that closeness can you embrace this experience. Joseph said to his brothers for them not to be angry with themselves because what they meant for evil to him God had used for good. (See Genesis 50:20.) I truly, without doubt, share that sentiment that what was meant for evil to me has benefited me and turned out for my good.

In order to help you to understand that no matter how storm-damaged or problem-ridiculed your life may be at this present time, restoration is possible. I want us to talk a bit more about Samaria of biblical times. In Jesus' day, Samaria had undergone some of the worst things possible. It had been besieged by the King of Syria, and there was a great famine (2 Kings 6:24). The famine and destruction in the land was so great that even the King of Samaria said these chilling words: "If the Lord does not help you, where can I find help for you?" The prophet Elijah also went to Samaria to present himself to Ahab whose wife was Jezebel, and she had massacred the prophets of the Lord (1 Kings 18:2–4).

As you can see, some of the things that happened to Samaria were not good kind things at times. Keep in mind that according to Bible history in Jesus' day the Samaritans were really the prior Israelites from the Northern Kingdom split. Bible history further states that after captivity ended many Israelites remained in Samaria and thus were given in marriage and other lifestyles to the forbidden. There was a widespread worship of foreign gods because of the mixture from other nations. By the time the Jews actually returned to rebuild the temple, the Samaritans, or Israelites from this section of the country, were not allowed to participate in the rebuilding (Ezra 4:2). Some of my studies reveal that the relationship between Samaria (Israel in the northern region) and Judah (in the southern region) continued to decline even until the time of Jesus' ministry. The reason I take special time to mention this is because I want to stress that Samaria was a region that had been plagued with many failures and to a degree even ownership of kingdom benefits were denied them. Their own kinsmen had frowned upon them, not allowing participation in rebuilding of the temple (Neh. 4; Ezra 4). Yet Jesus, the Scriptures tell us, "must needs to go through Samaria" (John 4:4, KJV). Even when the Samaritans rejected Jesus, He still visited that place. This should give you hope that no matter what you are going through and no matter how bad you think things look, the "must needs to go through Samaria" is crying out on your behalf. The "must needs" to be restored, fully restored, is here. It is up to you to either turn it away or do as the woman at the well did—recognize who it is that says to you *drink* so that you will thirst not nor go to the wrong places to draw renewed life again (John 4:15). Provide the will, and God will do the planting.

Don't fear your circumstances because fear is your greatest enemy and the devil's greatest weapon. Fear has no foundation in the spiritual fact world. Any facts that you can tie to your fears are only in the sense realm or the natural and cannot live in the supernatural realm. Denounce fear and go possess what has always been yours in the first place. Remember this is what David did when he went back to the enemy's camp and took back what had been taken from him (1 Sam. 30:18–19). I am afraid many people don't even know how to go to the enemy's camp and take back what was taken from them. Yet we sing the song over and over, "I'm going to the enemy's camp and take back what he stole from me." I cannot just sing a song unless I am determined to live it out in my life. So, here are a few tips to help you along your journey to take back what has been taken away from you.

First, realize who your opponent is. I have already concluded that you are living a saved life according to the Scriptures so let's go on. You must know who you are fighting before you set out to battle. Know and understand that the battle is the good fight of faith. That is the fight. Your faith is to rip through every barrier, every obstacle, and move every mountain out of your way. That is how you take back what was taken from you. David went physical in the enemy's camp. We go there with our faith leading the way. This is the victory that overcomes the world—our faith that is weapon enough. We are not fighting the *he* or the *she* or the people that did this or that to us; we are fighting a real devil, and it takes a real God to overthrow him. Never take fear to the battleground because you will lose with fear every time. Restoration and fear of obtaining cannot coexist. Fear of your circumstances and fear of your outcome must be surrendered to faith. Doubt and faith are not traveling companions. Where one is, the other is not there with it.

Plant your feet on the solid ground, and no matter what things look like or what they feel like, make sure you are established in God. Don't conveniently place your problems on the nightstand in your room or on the floor next to you. Cast all of your problems, abuses, misuses, lacks, deficiencies, and those other things too onto the Lord and do not go back to get them. Don't conveniently store them in your emotions so that you can pick them up anytime you like or consult with your problems again. I find those times would happen because I did not cast my cares very far. They were still with me when I started my day and when I ended my day. I was not whole at first. It seemed that life had thrown a fast enough and tough enough storm my way that it was always with me. That is when the Spirit of the Lord taught me how to forget those things that were behind. That was one of the best teaching days I have ever had. Just think, we can starve our past worries and give them nothing to live on, and they will die.

If you starve any living thing it will die. Your past pains and disappointments need your time, your worry, your emotions, and your attention to stay alive in your life. But if you starve them of those things and plant the good that is ahead, you instead learn to overcome. So one day I cast them so far that now I smile and laugh over the silly, weak times of my past. Jesus said, "Every kingdom divided against itself is brought to desolation, and every city or house divided against itself will not stand" (Matt. 12:25). So, don't be divided about whether you are going to apply the sure-proof restoration formula or not. Plant your mind to it! If you looked in your neighbor's garden and noticed that he had bigger, better, sweeter, and juicier fruits than you, wouldn't you want to know what you need to do differently in order to get that level of success with your garden? Well, take this formula as your method for growing the bigger, better, sweeter life by walking in total restoration.

I know we have repeated the steps a lot, but let's go there again: root out, pull down, destroy, throw down, build, and plant. These are the steps that lead to total restoration. I began to plant so much of the positive in my mind, my daily living, and everything that I did that some people began to think it was impossible to discourage me. Discouragement was not impossible for me to experience. It is just that when it came knocking at my door to remind me of the past I told it *those things don't live here anymore!* I just would not open the door for it. I had rooted out the old things that once lived there, and there were new occupants now. I had pulled down and thrown down everything not of use for my new journey to restoration. I was headed to the other side and I only planted those things that would assist me in getting there. I was loosed and I was headed somewhere. I was not loosed and wandering about unrestored. I had recognized that there is a process you must go through after you are loosed. There was a restoration that God declared He would bring his children into after their captivity had ended, and He did. He promised them good after the captivity ends (Jer. 29:10). Zechariah proclaimed:

> Sing and rejoice, O daughter of Zion! For behold I am coming and I will dwell in your midst, says the LORD.
> —ZECHARIAH 2:10

Jeremiah 31:3–4 states:

> Yes, I have loved you with an everlasting love; Therefore with lovingkindness I have drawn you. Again I will build you, and you shall be rebuilt.

It is for us today as spiritual Israel that we have too many promises to live in the bondage of the enemy. Why be heirs of such a great inheritance and not partake of it? Hebrews 6:17 tells us that we should have strong consolation who have fled for a refuge to lay hold on the hope that is set before us. Let no thing and no person and no self prevent you from experiencing through faith what God swore by oath. Surely, God will bless you, but you cannot have your blessings while you are stuck with your past pain and hurts.

Remember again that every tree the heavenly Father has not planted will be uprooted (Matt. 15:13). But if you let Him do all of it, no matter how painful to the flesh, you will be glad when you are on the other side of it. For years I would hear people talk about when things would get better, but in my mind I could not envision things as better. My captivity, bound in weakness, fears and doubt, obscured my vision and I could not see the victorious life that awaited me. At first, I could not see the "better times" or the abundance that comes when you just allow God to take care of you. He will take care of you and all your hurts, all the damage, all the mental and emotional turmoil. He will rebuild the land. He knows how you feel and He is touched by what we go through. This is why He needs to pass through your Samaria; your rejection, abandonment, and own lack of self worth, along with the abuses. He needs to pass through your Samaria because, if He does not, you will never be able to tell others, as I am telling you, to come see a man, the Man, Jesus Christ. Come see what He has told me about. Just being in His presence heals the past.

He passed through my Samaria, and now my land is different. The old weaknesses and crippling behavior that polluted me and caused me to join hand and hand with the abuse don't live here anymore. Those things have been rooted out and my mind has been conformed to the mind of Christ. Once there was an incident that changed what I worried about. My situation felt so bad to me that there were periods of time that I would worry. One day I walked into my sister's house and picked up a book. I don't even remember the name of the book. I just remember that when I opened the book the sentence read like this, "Have you ever seen a worried bird?" They don't even worry or concern themselves about where their next meal will come from, they just fly around like they have it made. Are we not more important than they? After reading that I decided I would let someone else worry about how I was going to get out of the abuse I was in. I decided to do like the birds; just go around like I had it made because I really did.

Don't worry about how you will turn the abuse cycle off. Just listen and you will hear that small, still voice directing your steps down the hall of strength and courage. Plant His directions for your life in your heart. We are to "be called trees of righteousness, The planting of the Lord, that He may be glorified" (Isa. 61:3). If the proper planting has not been done within us, then things will continue to spring up and choke our lives. For a long time doing these positive things were far too difficult for me. I wish I could tell you that I just jumped right in and listened to everything in one day and did it all. I wish I could say that I never cried about my ashes and I never worried. I can't say those things. For a time I was scared almost lifeless. I was so frightened that some days I could not even drive my car to work. There were days I pulled over to the side of the road just to get a hold of myself so I could continue on. For years I spent most of my lunchtime in the car crying about what had been done to me. But I came to my senses, called on my God, and rooted out the messes that had crippled me. I started going to lunch like a normal person. Everyone else was able to eat, so why shouldn't I? The only thing my stress did was make me lose a couple dress sizes, which paid off in the long run. I was waiting on God to help me and God was waiting on me to see the help that He had already put in my path.

Once I got so mad with a pastor on a Sunday afternoon when he said something that was way, way above my head. Now I use it all the time. Not because the pastor said it, but because I have put it into action and proved it in my own life. The pastor that day said, "God is not going to do any more for you than He has already done." Well, I thought: *He had better do more for me than He has done because there is a lot still that needs to be done. Can't God see the mess I am in? And what is this about Him not doing any more for me than He has already done?* Yes, everything I needed from Him I learned later was truly already done. I just needed to apply those things to my life. I needed to be the conqueror He destined me to be. I needed to not cast away my confidence. I needed to embrace the scripture that says I can ask what I will and it shall be done (John 15:7). Yes, all of what I needed had been already done and I soon found it out as I applied the principles. So I started rooting out some stuff from my life, pulling down the wrong that was displayed, and destroying the strongholds and I found out it worked. He did not do anything else; all of it had already been done. A new Jesus did not come and do it over. I took what Jesus had already done for me and applied it. I planted over and over the right godly things in my garden. I replaced every wrong done against me with right words, right thoughts, and right actions. I was being restored and it felt very, very good.

The place where I had arrived could only be accomplished by the revelation of the plan and steps that would afford me restoration, totally. Nothing of the past mattered anymore. I had no anger about it. In fact, I barely had any thoughts about it. The pain and anguish with the horrors from the abuse I felt were not on the inside or the outside. Newness of life had taken over and was being planted where fear and dismay had ruled. I planted kindness where anger once lived. I planted forgiveness where vengeance had ruled. I smiled more now than ever before because I realized those things had not taken me out. My life was forming into the likeness of the "tree planted by the rivers of water, That brings forth its fruit in its season, Whose leaf also shall not wither; And whatever he does shall prosper" (Ps. 1:3). I would have lost heart, unless I had believed that I would see the goodness of the Lord in the land of the living. Wait with expectations of God showing up! "Wait on the Lord; Be of good courage, And He shall strengthen your heart; Wait, I say, on the Lord!" (Ps. 27:14).

Chapter 10

Restoration Totally

IF IT HAD not been for the Lord who was on my side, my many challenges and obstacles, along with the pain and abuses of life, would have swallowed me up. Praise God, my "soul has escaped...from the snare of the fowlers; The snare is broken, and [I] have escaped" (Ps. 124:7). This scripture expresses King David's view of the Lord's defense of His people. My help came from the Lord.

Once total restoration is a part of your life it must be guarded and protected. Remember, the enemy will try to return and revisit you with those strongholds that once lived there. Don't let them in. "The secret of the Lord is with those who fear Him, And He will show them His covenant" (Ps. 25:14). When we are fully whole or restored we can walk in true covenant. You should never have to convince anyone you are restored and healed. It will show if you are. When a house is restored all that pass by can see and behold what has been done and that the property has been changed from the rundown state it was in. This is how God works. You don't have to talk it. Divine restoration can be seen if you live it out. Whatever you are restored to has your attention and your heart, and what you are restored from no longer has ownership of any part of you.

First of all, you will know when the restorative plan of God is working in your life, and you will know when it is not. Congratulations on both counts because it is a good thing to know either. You should not despair if you are not there yet because that is the first step in getting there: knowing where you are. Remember, I told you at the beginning that I was one of the most hopeless cases ever. People around me could not even see how I avoided the institutions because of a nervous breakdown that I never had. As I look back, I don't think what was done to me was nearly as bad as how I emotionally responded to it. Wow, I just don't believe that was me who said that! Those pains were real. Those sleepless nights, months, and years really happened. The stress and the extreme weight loss and the sicknesses were all truly real. What is wrong with me then in saying that my real problem was not what was done to me but what I did not do about it? Well, how about that! I could have had less pain and less horror, more healing and more peace had I responded differently.

Once you experience the hand of restoration on your emotional and spiritual life you will love being there and will be careful not to take any risks that would jeopardize what God has done in your life. Now let's make sure you understand me. To quote Paul again: "Not that I have already attained, or am already perfected; but press on, that I may lay hold of that for which Christ Jesus has also laid hold of me" (Phil. 3:12). I truly do not count myself to have apprehended anything but this: I know I have forgotten those things that are behind, they have no hold on me, and I am reaching forward to those things that are ahead. The things I reach forward to are the things which allow me keep experiencing the feeling of being divinely restored from my past and all of its ill damages. I do know that had it not been for the hardships of my past I could not know or have obtained what I have today. You know, if you change your route you change your scenery, and if you change your scenery you change your path and all that you have come to know and be.

When a person walks in restoration totally they are no longer terrified of their adversaries. Knowing Him and the power of His resurrection makes full restoration possible for anyone willing to pay the cost. The cost is only a willing, obedient heart. Don't run to the nearest exit, just listen and you may hear what Elijah heard when he ran from Jezebel. (See 1 Kings 19.) He ran and hid in a cave and God's voice said, "What are you doing here, Elijah?" (1 Kings 19:9). God's question to Elijah was not about a place, it was a question about condition. What are you doing here? As you continue each day down the path of total restoration you will become more and more acquainted with the exceeding abundance obedience brings. Your faith is the companion needed if ever you plan to reach it. Without faith you can't get there. There may be a lot of bumps and potholes and dangers as you journey, but faith in Him who has never lost a battle will pay off.

One of the most encouraging Bible stories I read over and over during my journey to becoming restored was the story of King Jehoshaphat. (See 2 Chronicles 20.) What I liked most about this Bible truth is that King Jehoshaphat (and I also) knew that the battle that was about to occur was too great for him. I knew that armies much greater than I were coming for me.

> Then the Spirit of the Lord came upon Jahaziel...in the midst of the assembly. And he said, "Listen, all you of Judah and you inhabitants of Jerusalem, and you, King

Jehoshaphat! Thus says the Lord to you: 'Do not be afraid nor dismayed because of this great multitude, for the battle is not yours, but God's.'"
—2 CHRONICLES 20:14–15

I am glad that I finally learned through truth that I did not have to be afraid or dismayed. Everything we are faced with is the Lord's battle to fight for us and on our behalf. But He will only fight for us if we allow Him. It feels so very good to sit back, relax, and allow Him to take care of me. Allowing Him to fight my battles and provide for me saves me energy for the things I should do in life.

No matter what your need is or your circumstances, know that your "redeemer liveth" (Job 19:25, KJV). If your Redeemer lives, allow Him to redeem you from the storms. You must persevere up the path to restoration. Never forget the formula: root out, pull down, destroy, throw down, build, and plant. God knew it would work for the nations and for Israel. Each step and each of the instructions or actions had a specific purpose within the blueprint for restoring. None of them could be omitted and ultimate results still be achieved.

After being divinely restored, there will be times when you will not understand yourself. Sometimes the way I respond to events that occur is not me at all and it feels weird. I actually know how to be strong and still let Him fight my battles for me. God promised that part of His restorative plan would be to heal the land, with water flowing in the desert places to build you up again. How about that? Water flowing in the desert! Watch the desert places of your life begin to fill in with peace, joy, and goodness as you draw nearer and nearer to Him. Restored does not mean you or I have it all, it just means that we have all we need to be whole.

You absolutely must "fight the good fight of faith" if you are to be successful according to the plans God has for your life (1 Tim. 6:12). This is why Jeremiah told God's people before the captivity ended: "For I know the thoughts that I think toward you, says the Lord, thoughts of peace and not of evil, to give you a future and a hope" (Jer. 29:11). He knew that even though they would soon be released (because the seventy years would be over soon), he gave them something to have faith and hope in. He reminded them that God had good thoughts about them and not evil and that He would bring them to their expectations. You must know this in some form or another. But you must be convinced of His good plans and love for you. When life has dealt you some sharp, piercing blows you will require proper healing for restoration.

Each day I still have to demonstrate the restoration God has embraced my life with. During work, my family life, and all other events I still recognize that being restored is precious enough to guard and cherish it by making right decisions and doing the godly thing whenever the opportunity arises. You must always operate in the realm of divine restoration. If not, you will walk in the influence of your abusive past.

When you are brought back from a place of captivity things have to be brought together properly in your life or you will move too fast. I share this story of restoration for two reasons only. First, God has told me to deposit this journey into your life. Secondly, it tastes too good not to share it. Who hath seen this house in its first glory, and how do you see it now? (Haggai 2:3) Don't get stuck on what the house used to look like. After the plan of divine restoration the latter shall be greater and brighter than the former.

Don't sit around wondering where all the things to rebuild will come from. There is no need to frustrate yourself over how will you get the things done in your life to be whole again. God spoke through the prophet Haggai when the people were very worried about how they were going to get what was needed to rebuild the temple in the natural sense. The people were concerned and so God reminded them that He would shake things up, and all things would come to fill the temple, the silver and the gold. The English Standard says that the treasures of all nations will come in, and His house will be filled with glory. This is tremendous for us; spiritual Israel, listen up! Let me explain how this relates to us. God is saying that He will shake up things in heaven and on earth, on the sea and on dry ground so that all treasures from other nations will find their way to you and me so that His house (people) will be filled with glory! Usually, you can listen to your life if you really want to know if you are walking in healing and wholeness. Are all things pertaining unto life and godliness finding you and your life filled with glory? You can answer the question for yourself. Life will let you know by what you allow and disallow in your life. Restored folks don't do certain things. We know who we are, and we demonstrate in our living the power of divine restoration. Live the life of Jacob. He did not and would not let the angel go until he got the blessing. He emerged from his struggle with the angel a person of victory no longer giving way to the heel-grabbing person he once was. Don't let go until God blesses you with what you came for. It may seem difficult as it was for me many times, but stay until He blesses. You must be serious and committed to receive or you never will; if you sway back and forth and are double minded about this, as the Word says, you will receive nothing (James 1:7). I hear something, don't you? I hear the Lord proclaiming Jeremiah 29:11:

> For I know the thoughts that I think toward you, says the LORD, thoughts of peace and not of evil, to give you a future and a hope.

I hear the Spirit saying:

> The glory of this latter house shall be greater than of the former.
>
> —Haggai 2:9

> Call to Me, and I will answer you, and show you great and mighty things, which you do not know.
>
> —Jeremiah 33:3

> Do not remember the former things, nor consider the things of old. Behold, I will do a new thing. Now it shall spring forth...I will even make a road in the wilderness.
>
> —Isaiah 43:18–19

There is a road for you already laid out that will spiritually guide you right out of the wilderness of your mind, spirit, and emotions. The road is called *restoration totally,* and it is calling you and me to be its travel companions.

> When the Lord brought back the captivity of Zion,
> We were like those who dream [live out your dream].
> Then our mouth was filled with laughter,
> And our tongue with singing.
> Then they said among the nations...
> The Lord has done great things for us,
> And we were glad
>
> —Psalms 126:1–3

Restoration Totally Experienced!

To Contact the Author

Send testimonials, requests for information, or book orders to:

Restoration Totally Sources
c/o Yvonne Mallory
P.O. Box 962
Uniontown, OH 44685

Web site: www.destinymine.com

E-mail: destinym@destinymine.com or
destinytovictory@aol.com